confident christian
6 Lessons on Apologetics for Teenagers

Group
(†) simply youth ministry

Confident Christian

6 Lessons on Apologetics for Teenagers

Copyright © 2009 Group Publishing, Inc.

www.group.com
www.simplyyouthministry.com

Credits

Contributing Authors: Mike DeVries, Karl Leuthauser, Dave Ricketts, Siv M. Ricketts, Christina Schofield, Mike Van Schooneveld, Vicki L. O. Witte, and Paul Woods

Editors: Kelli B. Trujillo and Mike Van Schooneveld

Chief Creative Officer: Joani Schultz

Copy Editor: Lidonna Beer

Art Director/Designer: Veronica Lucas

Cover Art Director: Jeff A. Storm

Cover Designer: Jeff A. Storm

Illustrator: Jeff A. Storm

Production Manager: DeAnne Lear

Scripture quotations are taken from the Holy Bible, New Living Translation, copyright © 1996, 2004. Used by permission of Tyndale House Publishers, Inc., Wheaton, Illinois 60189. All rights reserved.

ISBN 978-0-7644-3894-3

Printed in the United States of America.

10 9 8 7 6 5 4 3   18 17 16 15 14 13 12 11

Table of Contents

Introduction **1-2**

Is "Good" Really Good Enough? **3-21**
Why being a "good person" has almost nothing to do
with the gospel of Jesus Christ.

Who Needs a Savior? **23-45**
Why Jesus and his death are needed for salvation.

Will the Real God Please Stand Up? **47-67**
Why all roads don't reach the same destination.

Inherited Salvation **69-85**
Why no one can be born saved.

All God's Children **87-109**
Why believing in God just isn't enough.

Unorthodoxy **111-133**
Why the secrets of the cults can't compare
to true Christianity.

Foreword

By Greg Stier

Jesus' revolutionary message of salvation by grace gets easily garbled in today's tolerant, feel-good, all-paths-lead-to-God pop culture.

Today's teenagers are encouraged to believe in a God of their own making—a God who's been conveniently custom-designed to fit their own personal preferences. They might view God as anything from the "Great Barista in the Sky" who's expected to whip up whatever their hearts desire, to the "Great Teddy Bear in the Sky" who cheers them on as they pursue their own personal agendas, chasing after pleasure and success.

This generation's view of salvation is often custom-designed as well. God will likely divvy out eternal life to all who "tried their best," much like recreational league soccer trophies. Only ultra-evil characters such as Adolf Hitler and Osama bin Laden need to be concerned when the time comes for a final reckoning.

But Jesus' message of salvation is too vitally important for our teenagers to get it wrong! As youth leaders we must find fresh, creative, compelling ways to clearly communicate the truth from God's Word about salvation through faith in Jesus. And we must motivate and mentor our kids to share this message of hope and grace with their friends who struggle with cutting or addiction or relational conflict.

The six lessons in *Confident Christian* will help you do just that by encouraging your teenagers to sift through many of the conflicting views about God and salvation that swirl around them. *Confident Christian* will help you plant your kids' feet

firmly on a biblical foundation of truth. Through these well-crafted lessons, they'll learn how the Christian faith differs from the other major world religions. They'll see firsthand how our God's way of grace differs so dramatically from the way of works found in virtually every other religion or cult.

I am impressed and excited by the depth of the resource you hold in your hands. There is plenty of meat here for your students to chew on. For too long we've been spoon-feeding our teenagers Christianity-lite. And they've been getting eaten alive by their Philosophy 101 professors when they leave youth group and head off to college. Through role-playing, experiences, and interactive discussions, this curriculum will provide your teenagers a solid footing for discussing Jesus' message of salvation with anyone, anywhere. And each lesson's hands-on activities and life applications will powerfully and practically unlock Jesus' way of grace in their hearts, as well as their minds.

Without a firm biblical understanding of God and his free gift of salvation, is it any wonder that our teenagers struggle to explain the "hope they have within them" to their lost and hurting generation? Using this resource, you can dig deep right alongside your kids as you lead them into the spiritual truths they need to deepen their faith and to, in turn, share it with their generation! Lives depend upon it.

Introduction

"Isn't being a good person enough to get you into heaven?"
"Don't Mormons, Muslims, and Christians all believe in the
same God?"
"Is Jesus really the *only* way to God?"

Ever had to answer questions like these? Your students are asking
them—directly or indirectly. They live in a world of spiritual
options, and research is showing that even Christian teenagers
are confused about what they believe. A **group** Magazine
survey of over 1400 teenagers (93 percent of whom considered
themselves to be Christians) found that more than one-third of
them weren't sure if the Bible was accurate in all of its teachings
or believed that it was inaccurate; nearly four out of 10 thought
Satan was just a symbol of evil, not a real spiritual being; and
about one in five believed that Jesus committed sins while he
lived on earth.

Teenagers have a very natural curiosity about spirituality and
others' religious beliefs—yet often this curiosity, coupled with
uncertainty about Christian beliefs, can cause students to be
spiritually pulled off track. Even the most solid Christian
students in your church may be a bit confused about how to
embrace their own faith in a culture where all beliefs are seen as
equally good and relatively similar.

Confident Christian features six lessons that will help you lead
your students through an exploration of popular spiritual ideas in
our culture and compare them to the basic beliefs of Christianity.
Each lesson includes the following components:

Leader Insight—Here you'll get lots of background
information about the false belief you're studying so you can be
equipped to answer students' questions.

1

Warm-Up—These activities and discussions will warm your students up to the topic at hand, helping them begin to process the issues in a fun and interesting way.

Investigating the Evidence—During this portion of each lesson, teenagers will engage with the popular heresy they're studying and will investigate how those beliefs compare to Christianity.

 Bible Focus—Here teenagers will dig into their Bibles and look closely at key Scripture passages that point them toward the truth.

Life Application—To conclude each study, students will consider how the knowledge they've gained can be applied to their own lives and their relationships with others.

As you review each lesson, you'll find that they're packed with info about various religious belief systems, so take some time each week to familiarize yourself with the material. Pay special attention to the helpful hints in the **Leader Tips** and use the **Basic Belief Charts** (pgs. 136-143) and **For Further Research** ideas (pgs. 144-145) to expand your knowledge of the topics at hand.

Searching for the Truth
You may encounter some tough questions from students during these studies, but that's OK. In fact, that's *good*. As your students really begin to wrestle with the issues, they'll be chiseling out their own faith with confidence—defining it, exploring it, and coming to terms with it in a personal way. It is through questioning that students will really build a firm foundation for their Christian faith. It is through the searching that students will come to know the way, the truth, and the life: Jesus (John 14:6).

Introduction

Study 1

Is "Good" Really Good Enough?

Why being a "good person" has almost nothing to do with the gospel of Jesus Christ.

Matthew 9:9-13; John 4:23-24 and 14:6

The Lesson at a Glance

Study Sequence	Minutes	What Teenagers Will Do	Supplies
Warm-Up	10 to 15	**The Good, the Bad, and the Ugly**—Create a wall mural representing our culture's philosophy about being a "good" or "bad" person.	Magazines, scissors, tape, several pads of adhesive notes, pens, prepared posters
Investigating the Evidence	15 to 20	**Faith Facts**—Explore the "gospel of good works" and add more to the mural representing other religions' views; discuss why some people prefer a works-based faith.	Bibles, several pads of adhesive notes, pens, "Faith Facts" handouts (p. 20), prepared posters
Bible Focus	15 to 20	**Just One Way**—Explore what the Bible says about salvation and change the mural to represent that truth; open unappealing gifts and consider the types of worship that truly please God.	Bibles, a paper cross, tape, gift-wrapped boxes with unappealing items inside
Life Applicaion	up to 10	**Think-Fast Theology**—Think of ways to respond to the gospel of good works in challenging situations.	"Think-Fast Theology" handout (p. 21)

Before the Study

Warm-Up:

- Gather a variety of teen, pop culture, and news magazines such as *Seventeen*, *People*, *Entertainment Weekly*, *Sports Illustrated*, and *U.S. News and World Report*; you'll need one magazine for every two teenagers in your group.

- Set out the magazines and pairs of scissors on the floor or at various tables in your meeting area. You'll also need to make two signs on poster board, one with the title "Good People" on one side and "Heaven" on the reverse, and another with "Bad People" on one side and "Hell" on the reverse.

- Tape the signs to a prominent wall in your meeting room with the "Good People" and "Bad People" sides facing out. Be sure to leave a space of about 5 feet (or more) between the signs. *Also, set several rolls of tape on the floor near the signs.*

- Finally, be sure to have several pads of adhesive notes and a bunch of pens ready to pass out to the group.

Investigating the Evidence:

 Faith Facts:
Photocopy the **"Faith Facts"** handout (p. 20) and cut it into fours. You'll need several copies of each numbered segment.

Bible Focus:
Cut a large cross out of construction paper and have
some tape ready to affix it to the wall as you teach. Also,
colorfully gift-wrap several unappealing items, such
as a rock, an ugly tie, dryer lint, or a can of spinach for
participants to open during the activity.

Life Application:

 Think-Fast Theology:
Photocopy the **"Think-Fast Theology"** handout (p. 21)
and cut it apart; you'll need one segment of the handout
for every two teenagers in your group.

Leader Insight

This study tackles the "gospel of good works"—the belief that people can earn or work their way to salvation. Almost every religion and cult worldwide preaches some version of this teaching, since virtually every religion has some sort of moral code or list of religious practices that its adherents are required to fulfill. In its most oppressive forms, followers find themselves crushed under an endless list of duties they must perform. All of these ideologies share a belief that all people are imperfect and that we all must do something to make ourselves worthy of salvation under our own power.

A great example is the concept of "karma." According to this idea, people who do good things experience "good karma"—positive results. Conversely, those who do bad things experience "bad karma," their comeuppance, their just desserts. This is an increasingly pervasive and popular way of looking at the world. Karma is a part of the Hindu belief system which holds that the good and bad deeds people store up in their lifetimes are returned to them in equal measure in their next lifetimes. It's a kind of cosmic justice system in which each person gets what he or she deserves in the end. Like karma, many other belief systems and worldviews teach that people who do good things end up attaining prosperity and salvation while people who do bad things suffer for their actions. It's the gospel of good works at its clearest.

The problem with this system of justice is that it isn't very *just*. Both the Bible and our experience teach us that good people often suffer and bad people often prosper. And as we struggle to follow all the rules, we begin to wonder just how much more it's going to take to make us perfect. The quest to measure up becomes such a burden, and people are so confused by all the different teachers telling them which way they should take, that more and more people are simply giving up. They still feel tied to the gospel of good works, but they've decided to believe that whatever way they choose for fulfilling the justice system will be good enough to earn their way.

Especially in these days of "tolerance," we're all encouraged to believe that, no matter what your faith is, all the good people have earned their ticket into heaven. When it comes to salvation, most people only like to believe in "good karma." As long as you're one of the "good guys" you're OK, and it's really only people like Hitler who have anything to worry about. As a culture, we've embraced the basic idea of karma, but we're very relaxed about how we apply it to ourselves, and we're all pretty sure that we're good enough—that we're on our way upward instead of downward.

But the Bible doesn't teach the law of karma—that a person's good deeds can gradually draw them upward like a self-inflated balloon floating up into the sky. And it certainly doesn't teach the easy-breezy application of moral judgment and approval that most of us are content with these days. The Bible teaches that there is a holy God with a perfect law of justice that only he, by his miraculous power and amazing sacrifice, can satisfy. Even the strictest efforts toward holiness aren't enough to earn our way into heaven. Reminding your group of this and enabling them to guard them against the fallacy of "good karma" is the goal of today's study.

The Good, the Bad, and the Ugly

Welcome teenagers as they arrive and direct them to pair up and sit by a magazine. Tell everyone how excited you are about the study you'll be doing together over the next six weeks and take a couple of minutes to pray for them.

THEN SAY:

Welcome to our court today, where we're going to decide who is the good, who is the bad, and who is the ugly. Each pair of you has a magazine and scissors. What you need to do is search through the magazines and find people who fit into one of these three groups and cut out their pictures or the story about them. People who you think are genuinely good people should go in your "good" pile. People who are bad should go in your "bad" pile. And your "ugly" pile should be for those people you can't fit into one group or another; imperfect people who don't really seem to be trying to be "good" but aren't really quite so awful as to be "bad people." Maybe their lives are a little bit ugly.

Once you've got at least two people for each category, come up to the wall and tape them near the sign that matches them. Tape the people from your "ugly" pile somewhere in the middle between the "Bad People" and the "Good People" signs.

When participants are done taping their people onto the wall, direct pairs to join up and form new small groups of four. Give each small group a pad of adhesive notes and some pens.

We're going to add a bit to our "Good, Bad, and Ugly" wall.

Give small groups the following instructions, allowing everyone to finish each task before you move to the next one.

1. As a group, brainstorm three more people who you'd consider to be the epitome of a "good person." They can be historical figures or people who are alive today. Write each name on its own adhesive note, then add them to the "Good People" area of our wall.

2. Together, come up with five different things that characterize a really good person. They could be specific actions, examples of things you've seen or heard of, or specific character traits. Write them each down on their own note, then add them to the "Good People" section.

3. Now come up with five things that a person couldn't do and be considered "good." What actions, attitudes, or character traits disqualify someone from being considered a "good person"? Write them each down, then add them to the "Bad People" part of the wall.

4. In your groups, brainstorm three people who you'd consider to epitomize what it means to be a really "bad person." Again, it can be someone from the past or the present. Write one on each note and add them to the "Bad People" area of our wall.

Once all these new names and traits have been added to your wall, invite everyone up to look and see what others have added. Then ask the whole group these questions:

- How well does our wall reflect the way our culture thinks? Explain.

- Would you change anything on our wall or add anything to make it reflect our culture's perspective even better? If so, what?

- Do you know anyone personally who thinks this way? Without sharing names, give an example of how you've seen this viewpoint reflected in others' lives.

tip Interested in learning more about how Hinduism compares to Christianity? Check out the Basic Beliefs Charts and the For Further Research suggestions on pages 136-145!

Investigating the Evidence

 Faith Facts

Take the "Good People" and "Bad People" signs down, flip them over, and tape them back up so "Heaven" and "Hell" are showing instead.

SAY:

Now put yourself in God's shoes. Imagine that you have to determine whether someone deserves to go to heaven or hell based on their good or bad deeds. Every single person has to go under one sign or the other. When you die, there's no "halfway to heaven" pile to land in. That means you all need to take all the people you put in the middle and move them either to the "Heaven" or "Hell" side of the wall.

Have the students go back up and each find one of the people in the "ugly" category they'd put on the wall and move it. Remind them that the categories they started with are still in force: They should only put people under the "Heaven" sign if they're truly good, and they should only put people under the "Hell" sign if they're truly bad. In this case, either the students will have to relax their standards of what they considered "good," or they'll have to expand their standards of what they considered "bad."

When they're done, **ask the group:**

- How did you decide who went into which pile, in the beginning?

- Do you feel that the people got what they deserved now that I've changed the signs to "Heaven" and "Hell"? Why or why not?

> ### tip
> One problem your group might run into is that in order to make their decision, either a lot of people got into heaven who didn't really deserve to be there and would surely cause problems, or only a few people were able to make it into heaven and a lot of people ended up in hell who weren't really terribly bad. Try not to get too sidetracked onto this if it comes up, and let them know that we'll be seeing what the Bible has to say about these problems in just a little while when we "investigate the evidence."

Have teenagers re-form their small groups of four. Then, within each small group, have them number off 1 through 4. Direct all the 1's to go to one corner of the room, all the 2's to go to the next corner, and so on. Give each corner group several copies of their corresponding section of the **"Faith Facts"** handout (p. 20). (The 1s get "Group 1: Faith Facts" and so on.) Also, give each corner group some adhesive notes and pens.

Explain that each corner group has some information about a specific religion or worldview. (Group 4 has information about several religions.)

Challenge corner groups to read their handout together, and then brainstorm and write down more traits on adhesive notes that describe how a person gets to heaven or what prevents a person from going to heaven according to their assigned worldview. (They should write the name of the religion or worldview on each note.)

Give corner groups about five minutes to read their handout, then create notes and add them to the wall by the "Heaven" or "Hell" signs.

When all the corner groups are done, instruct everyone to return to their original small groups of four.

SAY:

You've each learned a little about other religions and worldviews. Now take turns quickly teaching the others in your small group what you learned; you've each got just one minute.

After four or five minutes, lead teenagers in a small group discussion in their groups of four, asking these questions and allowing time for them to talk through them together.

- Imagine you lived according to the beliefs of a works-based religion. How would that change the way you feel about yourself and others?

- Why do you think so many people believe that you need to earn your place in heaven?

- Why do you think people might find the idea of working their way into heaven attractive?

- How easy do most people think it is to earn their way into heaven? Explain.

Have everyone look back toward the wall as you verbally highlight some of the things written there, summarizing what the group has created.

You've done a great job putting together a representation of what many people believe and what many religions teach—what we'll call the gospel of good deeds. Christianity is different from every other religion in this way: We are accepted by God because of God's grace, not because of what we say or do. Most religions require people to make some sort of sacrifice to God. Only in Christianity does God extend a sacrifice to humanity: Jesus. Let's explore together more of what the Bible says about this.

 Bible Focus

Just One Way

Invite volunteers to read the following passages aloud: Romans 3:10-18, Romans 3:23, and Isaiah 64:6. Then read Romans 6:23a aloud: "For the wages of sin is death."

Summarize the point of these passages, pointing out that every single human being who has ever lived is sinful. That sin in our lives means we've earned "death"—separation from God and an eternity in hell.

As you explain this, call up some volunteers to help you remove any people who are by the "Heaven" sign and move them all to the "Hell" category.

SAY:

None of these people, no matter how good they are, are without sin. On their own, even these great people are sinners and "fall short of God's glorious standard" (Romans 3:23).

Now invite volunteers to read the following Scriptures aloud: Romans 6:23, John 3:16, and John 14:6.

Tape the paper cross you prepared next to the "Heaven" sign.

SAY:

The only way a person can get to heaven, no matter how "good" or "bad" they seem, is through Jesus. Jesus died on the cross to pay for our sin—he paid the penalty we each deserved. When we accept the forgiveness Jesus offers and put our faith in him, then we can go to heaven.

Select one of the good people now on the "Hell" side of the sign.

SAY:

The only way this person can go to heaven is if he accepts Jesus' gift of grace and forgiveness. Then move the person to the "Heaven" side of the sign.

Repeat this again with another example from the "Hell" side.

Then select a very bad person from the "Hell" side or mention an example of your own (such as Adolf Hitler or Osama Bin Laden).

SAY:

Even this person can be forgiven by Jesus. Jesus' grace is that big. If this person repented of his sin, accepted Jesus' grace, and committed his life to Jesus, even he would go to heaven. Move that person to the "Heaven" category.

Ask the group:

• What's your gut reaction to what I've just explained? Why?

• What might someone find difficult to accept about what the Bible teaches? Explain.

• What's freeing about this way of viewing things?

After participants have had a chance to share their reactions...

SAY:

So does this mean that there's no point to being good? Shouldn't we try to live right? Let's explore this a bit more.

Ask a volunteer to read Matthew 9:9-13 aloud. Then hand out several gift-wrapped boxes filled with items that teenagers would never want, such as a rock, an ugly tie, dryer lint, or a can of spinach. Ask volunteers to open the gifts as you read aloud the following situation.

SAY:

Imagine your aunt and uncle arrive at your house on your birthday. They hand you a huge gift, beautifully wrapped, and you can't wait to tear into it. You rip off the paper, filled with anticipation. You are dying to see what's inside! They are grinning from ear to ear. "We saved up for months to be able to buy this for you," they say, adding to the excitement. Your face falls when you see inside, and even though you try, you can't mask your disappointment when you see you have just been given the complete, 500-volume video series of the Lawrence Welk Show. *It must have cost them hundreds of dollars.* "You shouldn't have," you say, and you mean it. It's obvious they really have no idea what you are like or what you want from them.

Ask:

- Looking at this example, how do you think God feels when people offer him gifts that are completely inappropriate or fall so far short of what he really wanted?

Have volunteers read Hosea 6:6 and Isaiah 29:13 aloud and invite the group to summarize what these passages mean.

Then have volunteers read Ephesians 2:8-10 and James 2:18 aloud and ask the group to contrast the point of these passages with the first two.

Ask:

- Imagine a friend asked you, "What does God really want from us?" Based on what we just read, what would you say?

After teenagers have shared their ideas,
God has made it easy for people to be made right with him—not through rituals or sacrifices, but through Jesus. We respond by accepting this gift and relying entirely on his grace. We are continually changed by Jesus and we strive to live a life that pleases him.

Let's consider ways we can share the truth of Christ with our friends who believe heaven is for "good people."

Life-Application

 Think-Fast Theology

Have teenagers re-form their four corner groups from earlier in the study. Give each corner group a scenario from the **Think-Fast Theology** Handout (p. 21) and challenge them to work together to come up with a response to someone who believes that "doing good" leads to salvation. Give the corner groups some time to think over their responses. Then have them take turns delivering their answer for the scenario to the entire group.

After you've finished playing the game, take some time to discuss these questions with the large group:

• Have you ever tried to share your faith with someone who believes doing good things is the way to get to heaven? What was your experience like?

• Why is it so hard to share your faith with someone who practices a works-based faith?

• What does Christianity have to offer that the "gospel of good works" doesn't?

• What are some good ways we can start conversations about our faith with friends who don't believe in grace-based Christianity?

• Which Bible verses might be helpful to remember when talking to your friend who believes that heaven is for "good people?"

Take a moment to emphasize the importance of showing respect to other worldviews while sharing the truth in love.

SAY:

It is important to be tolerant of people who believe differently than you do and to not look down on them. But it is also impossible to genuinely care for someone and yet not want to help them understand the truth about Christ. As Christians we believe that the grace found in Jesus is the only way to be made right with God.

Ask:

- Is it possible to express disagreement with someone's worldview without offending them? Explain.

- What do you think will most attract your unsaved friends to Christianity? Why?

Close by inviting teenagers to form pairs and pray for their friends of different faiths (or no faith at all).

 **GROUP 1:** Faith Facts

Karma and the Law of Reincarnation

Hindus believe in a class system where everyone is part of a higher or lower class. Karma is the Hindu moral law of cause and effect—good actions lead to rebirth into a higher class; bad actions result in suffering or lower class in the next life.

The first step toward salvation is philosophy or knowledge, the second step is through works of religious observance like meditation and other religious acts, and the third step is devotion through worshipping images or idols. People who fail to live upright lives according to Hindu laws will be rewarded by suffering and by being reincarnated as a member of a lower class or even an animal. People who are born into a lower class are given no pity for their circumstances and are treated with disdain, because Hindus believe those people are only getting what they deserve from their previous life. From the Hindu perspective, life is a kind of curse where you have to work for your salvation, lifetime after lifetime, gradually working your way up, until at the end you escape the cycle of pain and are made free by becoming one with God, at which point your self is eradicated and ceases to exist as an individual.

 **GROUP 2:** Faith Facts

The Five Pillars of Islam

Muslims believe there are five pillars to achieving salvation and a holy life. First, recite the profession of faith, preferably many times: "There is no god but Allah, and Muhammad is his prophet." Second, perform the *salat* prayer 5 times a day while facing Mecca. Third, donate regularly to charity; at least the minimum of a 2.5% zakat charity tax. Fourth, fast during the month of Ramadan. Fifth, make at least one pilgrimage to Mecca.

Islam is a religion that draws no lines between the sacred and the secular, and breaking a social law is as bad as breaking a religious law. In the same way, religious laws (such as rules about modesty) have the power of social laws and are subject to harsh punishments.

 **GROUP 3:** Faith Facts

The Noble Eightfold Path of Buddhism

Buddhists believe that life is defined by the four noble truths: (1) Life is suffering, (2) there is a cause for suffering (desire), (3) there is a way to make suffering end (by eliminating desire), and (4) there is a path that leads to the end of suffering. That path is the Noble Eightfold Path. The Noble Eightfold Path is: Right Views, Right Motive, Right Speech, Right Action, Right Livelihood, Right Effort, Right Mindfulness, and Right Contemplation.

In order to achieve salvation, you must always have the right beliefs, you have to say the right things, you have to have the right motives, you have to avoid doing all the wrong things (like lying, cheating, stealing, and self-indulgence), you have to be making the right kind of effort and be thinking of yourself in the right way, you have to spend your time doing the right things. The goal is complete elimination of the self, because the self is what leads to desire, and desire is what leads to pain. Only complete elimination of the self will lead to nirvana (salvation).

 **GROUP 4:** Faith Facts

Other Global Religions

Old Testament Judaism held that you had to sacrifice constantly and follow the tenets of the law to get forgiveness for your sins. Modern Jews don't sacrifice, but the orthodox Jewish law starts from a base of 613(!) commandments about how a Jew should live his or her life and goes from there.

Ancient pagan religions like those of the Romans and Greeks held that you had to attend certain festivals and make certain sacrifices to the gods to achieve salvation. Other religions, including many in South America, Central America, India, China, Mesopotamia, northern Europe, and West Africa practiced human sacrifice as part of their religion, some of them right up into the 19th century and beyond. Jehovah's Witnesses believe that only 144,000 people will receive salvation and must work to ensure that they're part of that small number.

Confucianism, though it is more of a philosophy than a religion, prescribes a routine for life based on ritual, performance of social duties, respect for your ancestors, loyalty to your rulers, and being gentlemanly. Many non religious people today still hold to a religious ideology of some type in the sense that they believe good people go to heaven or receive some sort of reward here on earth for their goodness.

THINK-FAST THEOLOGY

At a slumber party, Maggie and her friend, Anna, have a heart-to-heart talk about their differing religious views. Anna says she thinks going to church on Sundays and being a good person is enough to get into heaven. Maggie shares what the Bible teaches about salvation.

THINK-FAST THEOLOGY

Steven tells his friend Josh that he's a Christian. Josh says that he doesn't think it matters what religion you are to get into heaven. We all come through different routes but we all end up in the same place. Steven responds.

THINK-FAST THEOLOGY

Brad's friend experiences an unexpected family tragedy and blames the incident on karma, thinking she has done something terrible to deserve this punishment. Brad responds.

THINK-FAST THEOLOGY

Madison's friend Ashley says that she doesn't believe a good God would ever send anyone to hell. Madison shares what the Bible has to say.

THINK-FAST THEOLOGY

Kayla invited her Jewish friend to a Bible study. Her friend was very quiet during the meeting, but afterward had many questions about Jesus. She was taught that Jesus was just a rabbi and did not rise from the dead and has nothing to do with a person's eternal state. Kayla responds.

Study 2

WHO NEEDS A SAVIOR?

Why Jesus and his death are needed for salvation.

2 Corinthians 5:21; John 8:12 and 11:25

The Lesson at a Glance

Study Sequence	Minutes	What Teenagers Will Do	Supplies
Warm-Up	up to 10	**One-Man Show**—Have participants try to untangle themselves from a human knot and compare their experience to religion with and without Jesus.	Blindfolds
Investigating the Evidence	15 to 20	**Generally Religious**—Explore what makes up a religion.	Bibles, dry-erase board or flip-chart and marker
Bible Focus	20 to 25	**One of a Kind**—Reveal hidden objects to illustrate the uniqueness of Christianity's focus on Christ.	Bibles; "Box Labels" handout (p. 43); 6 small boxes; the Koran; the Torah (or an Old Testament); a Hindu text; a Buddhist text; *The Analects of Confucius* or quotes from Confucius; a "picture" (painting or drawing) of Jesus; dry-erase board or flip-chart and marker

...chart continued on pg. 24

Study Sequence	Minutes	What Teenagers Will Do	Supplies
Life Application	**up to 20**	**Let's Get Personal—** Discover truths about Jesus' centrality in the Christian faith by doing science experiments with a partner.	Bibles; "Jesus-Free Faith?" handouts (pp. 44-45); eggs, cups, a large pitcher of water, salt, spoons; a large bowl of water, lots of tarnished pennies, soap, rags, several packets of Taco Bell Border Fire sauce or Tabasco sauce, paper towels; masking tape, cotton balls, candy prize

Before the Study

Warm-Up:

- Gather enough blindfolds for all of your teenagers. Anything will work, as long as participants won't be able to see through them.

Investigating the Evidence:

- You need a dry-erase board or a flip-chart and a marker.

 Bible Focus:
   You're going to need six small boxes (such as shoeboxes). Photocopy the **"Box Labels"** page (p. 43) and cut out the different labels. Tape the labels to the tops of boxes. Put the following items in the corresponding boxes: a copy of the Koran for Islam; a copy of the Torah for Judaism; a copy of the Vedas, the Puranas, or the Mahabharata for Hinduism; a copy of the *Tipitaka* or other collections of Buddha's writings; a copy of *The Analects of Confucius for Confucianism*; and a picture (such as a familiar painting or drawing) of Jesus for Christianity. Check your local library for copies of the books you need.

Life Application:

- You'll create three stations for this part of the study; at each station, place a few copies of the corresponding instructions from the "Jesus-Free Faith?" handouts (pp. 44-45). If possible, set up the stations far away from each other in your room (such as in three different corners).

- At Station 1, set out several eggs, several cups or glasses, salt, several spoons, and at least one pitcher of water.

- At Station 2, you'll need lots of tarnished pennies (at least one for each participant), a large bowl of water, some bars of soap, some rags, several packets of Taco Bell Border Fire sauce (or a few bottles of Tabasco sauce), and ample paper towels.

- At Station 3, you'll need cotton balls (one per participant) and masking tape. Mark out a "starting line" on the floor with tape and then make several more marks with tape, about one line every one or two feet. Be sure to have a final line that is a great distance away from the starting line—at least 10 feet but ideally 15 or 20 feet away. Set a candy prize at the farthest line.

---

tip If you can't get copies of the texts themselves, print out samples from the web. Check out these sites:

The Koran—
http://quod.lib.umich.edu/k/koran/browse.html

The Torah—www.biblegateway.com
(print something from the Old Testament)

Various Hindu Scriptures—
www.indiadivine.org/categories/Hindu-Scriptures/

Buddha's writings—
www.buddhanet.net/pdf_file/words_of_buddha.pdf

The Analects of Confucius—
www.wsu.edu/~dee/CHPHIL/ANALECTS.HTM

Leader Insight

For many people, the idea of a savior is an idea that they just don't like. And the whole idea of that savior being a flesh and blood person who lived and breathed and slept and died just doesn't fit into their neat little picture of religion. Even in many churches these days, the person of Jesus Christ is an unwanted guest.

The reasons people find the idea of a personal savior offensive come in all shapes and sizes. For some people, accepting the idea of a savior means admitting they actually need to be saved. For others it means letting in a person instead of just finding their place in a system of rules and rituals and Sunday potlucks—and they're not ready to get that personal. Some simply can't get over the apparent barbarism of finding salvation in the bloody torture and death of another human being, even a human who claimed to be God. And others simply can't swallow the realness of the whole thing and think Jesus must have just been an idea and his death was merely symbolic. Cut out the middle man, they say, and go straight to the deep spiritual concepts.

Plenty of people out there will be happy to tell your teenagers why they don't need Jesus—a real Jesus. Pretty much every other religion and philosophy in the world is doing so right now. All of them offer guaranteed ways to heaven without the need for a savior. You can be saved by being good, you can be saved by becoming enlightened, you can be saved by learning the secret, you can be saved by becoming a member, you can be saved just by being yourself. Every religion on earth is offering up these tempting falsehoods like a buffet in front of our noses.

But Christianity is completely unique out of all the religions of the world because we don't preach a path or a doctrine or a secret or a sect. We preach a person. Christianity isn't just one more religion among many because Christ isn't one more prophet or teacher among many. Christ unequivocally claimed to be God.

Jesus didn't come to earth to create another religion—Christianity—he came to save men and women from sin and give us new life. The problems of humanity go far beyond anything a mere religion could do for us. We see it every day in all the misery and trouble people still suffer even though we've had religious teachings for thousands of years. Only in the person of Christ and the radical transformation he offers us can we find rest for our souls. In today's study teenagers will confront the myth that mere religion can fill the hole that Jesus offers to heal and see what the Bible has to say about who Jesus really was.

Warm-Up

◊ One-Man Show

Take some time to greet teenagers as they arrive, then lead
the group in this challenge. Teenagers will need to stand up
and gather into a circle. (If you have lots of participants, you
may need to have them form two or more circles of 10 or 12
participants each.) Once they're in the circle, they need to reach
out and grab hands with two different people, one for each hand.
The tricky part is that they can't grab hands with either of the
people right next to them. Explain to your group that the goal of
the activity is to untangle themselves so they form an even circle
(sometimes you end up with two circles).

> **tip** There's a certain risk involved in doing any activity
> blindfolded. Make sure the area around the group is clear and
> make sure to keep an eye on them and keep them in check so
> no one gets hurt.

Right before the group starts, stop them and explain that they
have to complete the entire exercise blindfolded! Go up to each
of your teenagers and put the blindfolds on them, then tell them
they can begin. Allow everybody some time to try to untangle
themselves. After a few minutes of trying, tell them to stop and
push their blindfolds up so they can see.

Obviously it's not easy to untangle yourselves when you can't see. In fact, you're just as likely to hurt yourself or someone else as to get yourself free.

Explain that you're going to give them another chance. But this time you need a volunteer to step outside the circle and take off their blindfold. Once you have someone, have everyone get back into a circle and link up hands again, then push their blindfolds down so they can't see again. This time around the people in the circle have to follow the instructions of the person outside the circle. It's that person's job to tell the people in the circle what to do to untangle themselves.

When you're finished, have everybody sit down and discuss the following questions.

Ask:

- On a scale of 1 to 10—1 being "piece of cake" and 10 being "impossible"—how hard was it to disentangle the circle when you were blindfolded? Why?

- How would you rate the difficulty of the experience when you had somebody outside the circle giving instructions? Explain.

- Was there anything hard for you or frustrating about taking orders from someone outside the circle? Explain.

SAY:

A lot of people treat religion like the game we just played. Everyone is trying to untangle themselves from the problems we all have, but we can't see how to get ourselves out. Christianity is similar to when we had someone standing outside the circle who could see. Jesus is God, and Jesus lived a perfect life, so he knows what's wrong with us and he knows how to fix it. But asking any of the other founders of the other major religions is like asking one of the blindfolded people in the circle for help. How could they help us when they're just as caught up in the circle of human imperfection and confusion as we are?

Lots of people will tell you that you don't need a savior to be saved. But the Bible makes it clear that we need to be aware of our need for a savior and to find salvation in Jesus. Only Jesus, out of everyone who has ever lived, has really ever been outside the circle of human imperfection and confusion. In today's study we're going to look more closely at why Jesus is unique and why you can't be saved without a savior.

Investigating the Evidence

Generally Religious

Have teenagers form pairs and discuss these questions with each other:

- Why do you think some people reject the idea of Jesus as their personal savior?

- If you know anyone who thinks this way, what are their reasons?

Give pairs some time to brainstorm answers to this question and encourage them to come up with a variety of possible reasons. If teenagers need help getting started, ask them to think about what people don't like about Jesus' teaching, or what people have a hard time accepting about Jesus' story, or what people seem to prefer to Jesus.

After a few minutes, have everyone gather back together and turn toward the front. Invite teenagers to call out some of their ideas; as they do, write them on the left-hand side of your dry-erase board or flip-chart. Answers could be things like:

- *People don't want to admit they need a savior.*

- *People just want the social aspects of Christianity.*

- *People don't like how violent Jesus' story is.*

- *People want to find their own way to heaven.*

- *People think Jesus' story is symbolic and spiritual, not real.*

Ask the group:

- What are some substitutes for a savior—other ways to be "saved"—that people have come up with? Let's come up with as many as we can.

Again, jot down teenagers' answers on your dry-erase board or flip-chart right next to the previous list. (Be sure not to use up all your room!) Some answers might be:

- *You can be saved by being good.*

- *You can be saved by becoming enlightened or getting in touch with your "true self."*

- *You can be saved by learning the secret.*

- *You can be saved by becoming a member of a certain group.*

Ask:

- In your opinion, what does it take for ideas to be considered a religion?

Explain to the group that this is their chance to define what a religion should be like. For example, what important questions does it have to answer? What problems does it need to have solutions for? What kind of person should the founder be like?

Discuss these questions with your group to help them come up with their answers and list them in a third column on your dry-erase board or flip-chart.

SAY:

Plenty of people out there will be happy to tell you why you don't need Jesus. Pretty much every other religion in the world does exactly that. All of them offer guaranteed ways to heaven without the need for a savior. But Jesus offers something different from all those other religions. Let's take a look at why Christianity is so different from all the other religions.

Don't erase what you've written on the dry-erase board or flip-chart because you're going to add to it in the next section.

 Bible Focus

One of a Kind

For this part of the study you're going to need the labeled shoeboxes with the religious texts inside them. Set the boxes up so everyone can see them, but don't let them see what's inside!

SAY:

Each of these boxes represents a different major religion. And inside each box I've managed to capture the heart of each religion and what it preaches.

Invite six volunteers up to the front and have them pick up the boxes one at a time, read the labels and descriptions aloud, and then each try to guess what is inside their box. Then have each volunteer open up his or her box, one at a time, showing the group what's inside. Be sure to save the Christianity box for last. As teenagers open the boxes, explain that the various texts inside hold the stories and doctrines that make up the hearts of the different religions. When the last box is opened and the volunteer shows the group the picture of Jesus, **ask the group:**

· What were you expecting to find in this box?

· Why do you think there's a picture inside of this box instead of a Bible?

SAY:

Christianity is completely unique out of all the religions of the world, because we don't preach a path or a doctrine or a secret or a sect. We preach a person. Christianity isn't just one more religion among many because Christ isn't one more prophet or teacher among many. Let's look more closely at what's unique about Jesus.

Explain that in this part of the study they're going to be creating a resume for Jesus based on what the Bible has to say about him. Have teenagers form four groups and give each group a set of verses. Give them a few minutes to look up the verses and discuss what unique thing about Jesus the verses tell us. Be sure to let the groups come up with their own answers.

· Group 1: John 8:46 and 2 Corinthians 5:21 (Jesus claimed to be sinless.)

- Group 2: John 11:25 and John 6:54 (Jesus claimed to be able to save us from sin and death.)

- Group 3: Matthew 11:28 and John 8:12 (Jesus pointed to himself, not his teachings, as the solution.)

- Group 4: John 8:19, John 10:38, and John 14:9 (Jesus claimed to be God.)

Once all the groups have had time to go through their verses and come up with their answers, call everyone back together. Have the groups take turns reading their verses out loud and explaining what unique claim is made about Christ. Write their answers down on the far right-hand side of your dry-erase board or flip-chart next to the other lists you've created so far in the lesson. Check to make sure that the answers teenagers came up with roughly match what they were supposed to get out of the verses.

After you've had a chance to go through all four points, go back over them with the group and discuss them with the following questions.

—Jesus claimed to be sinless.

Ask:

- Do you think it's important for the founder of a religion to be a very good person, even perfect? Why or why not?

- How would it make you feel about a religion if you knew its founder wasn't able to live according to the rules they preached? Explain.

SAY:

If you've read the Old Testament you know what flawed people Abraham and Moses were. One was a liar and schemer and the other was a murderer. Yet they are two of the pillars of Judaism. The fact that Buddha had gone through multiple rebirths meant that he had lived numerous imperfect lives, and the story of his search for enlightenment is the story of someone searching for answers that he didn't have. Muhammad was married to 11 women and was asked to seek forgiveness for his sins in the Koran. No matter how important they were, none of these other religious founders came close to living the kind of life Christ did.

—Jesus claimed to be able to save us from sin and death.

Ask:

- Imagine you were asked to prove the existence of sin. What evidence would you offer? Why?

- What kinds of solutions have people and religions tried to come up with for the problem of sin?

- What about death? What solutions or explanations have people and religions come up with when it comes to death?

—Jesus pointed to himself, not his teachings, as the solution.

Ask:

- Based on what you've read and heard, how was Jesus' mission on earth different from other religious founders?

SAY:

Jesus didn't come to earth to create another religion—he came to save men and women from sin and give us new life. The problems of humanity go far beyond anything a mere religion could do for us. We see it every day in all the misery and trouble people still suffer even though we've had religious teachings for thousands of years. Only in the person of Christ and the radical transformation he offers us can we find rest for our souls.

—Jesus claimed to be God.

Ask:

- Jesus made a claim about himself that we either must believe or reject. How would it change your view of Jesus' teachings if he weren't really God—if it were just something he made up about himself? Explain.

- On the flip side, if Jesus *were* really God, how does that impact the way you read his teachings?

SAY:

No one else believes that their religion's founder is God. We cannot ignore Jesus' claim about himself and view him as some sort of mild, safe teacher with good sayings. We either must accept it or reject it. And if we reject his claim to be God, how can we take him seriously at all?

With most religions, there are many things that make sense and that "work." But none of them provide a savior. Perhaps like me, you know that there are things you've done that you can't make right. The power and truth of Christianity is grace. God offers forgiveness and grace for every sin we've committed, even if we can't make it right. Jesus paid for them. We can't be perfect people, but he can be perfect for us, and he can give us his own spirit to make us like him. We just need to have the strength to admit our need for him.

Life Application

 Let's Get Personal

Have everyone re-form their pairs from earlier in the study and direct teenagers' attention to the three stations you've set up in your room. Explain that they'll find instructions for an activity and some discussion questions at each station. Point out a clock in your meeting room and let them know they've got about 12 to 15 minutes total to visit all three stations and follow the instructions. (Station 2 will take longer than the others, so pairs should plan accordingly.) They can start at any station they want—they just need to do all three in the allotted time.

See if teenagers have any questions, then have them get started.

At Station 1, teenagers will see how salt added to water makes an egg buoyant. They'll use this experience to launch a discussion about having a "salty" faith rather than a watered-down faith.

At Station 2, teenagers will use hot sauce to clean tarnished pennies and will consider the difference between trying to "clean" one's life by one's own effort or being truly cleaned by Jesus.

At Station 3, teenagers will try to throw cotton balls. (They don't go very far!) They'll talk about how it is impossible to bridge the gap of sin and get to God by one's own efforts—we need Jesus.

After 12 to 15 minutes, have everyone gather back together and use some broad, open-ended questions to get teenagers to share their response to the experiences, such as "What stands out to you most from the stations? Why?" or "What did you get out of those experiences? Explain."

THEN SAY:

Many people have adopted parts of religions while disregarding other parts. This is especially true of Christianity. There are many people who believe the parts of Christianity that they like, but overlook other parts. This is especially true when it comes to Jesus—many people who call themselves Christians don't truly accept what Jesus said and did. They don't truly believe in him as their savior.

Ask:

- What would Christianity do for a person if he or she believed everything except the part about believing in Jesus? Do you think it would still be *Christianity?* Why or why not?

SAY:

You will definitely encounter Christ-less Christian thought and perspectives in the future. Most of these religions get by through offering people some of the valuable truths of Christianity without bringing in Christ. If they were completely false or foolish, they wouldn't be so popular. But it doesn't matter how much truth surrounds a deception, it is still a deception. They fail to see that we are all broken people who sin and need a personal savior.

I'm sure you will run into religious people who are good people and have spiritual passion. But if they don't have Christ, they don't have the truth.

Lead your teenagers in prayer, asking God to use them to help people in your community and around the world to realize their need for Jesus Christ.

BOX LABELS

✡ JUDAISM ✡

Judaism began when God called Abraham out from his home city in about 2000 B.C. Moses is the most important figure in the Jewish scriptures after Abraham and is credited with writing down the Torah, the Law, the first five books of the Old Testament (as Christians call it).

ॐ HINDUISM ॐ

Hinduism is an ancient and diverse religion of many gods that preaches belief in reincarnation, karma, and a class system and has no single founder.

✝ CHRISTIANITY ✝

You know what it is!

水 CONFUCIANISM 水

Confucianism is a Chinese ethical and philosophical system that was founded by Confucius, who lived and taught around 500 B.C. Confucianism is his attempt to lay out the principles for right living and an ordered society.

☪ ISLAM ☪

Islam was founded by the prophet Muhammad in the 7th century. Muslims believe that their faith is the restoration of the original faith of Abraham, which had been distorted by Jews and Christians.

☸ BUDDHISM ☸

Buddhism is based on the teachings of Siddhartha Gautama Buddha. Buddha left a life of royalty to seek enlightenment. Buddhism is an atheistic religion that preaches how to escape the pain of life by achieving freedom from desire.

JESUS-FREE FAITH STATION 1: Sinking Without Salt

With your partner, fill a glass halfway full with water, then stir in three spoonfuls of salt. When the salt has dissolved, carefully put an uncracked egg into the water…it should float. (If it doesn't take it out and stir in just a bit more salt.)

Imagine the salt in the water represents true faith in Jesus—and the egg represents you. Now think creatively with your partner:

• How can this experiment symbolize faith and the difference it makes in our lives?

Matthew 5:13 says, "You are the salt of the earth. But what good is salt if it has lost its flavor? Can you make it salty again? It will be thrown out and trampled underfoot as worthless."

•   What do you think it means for someone to lose their saltiness?

•   What examples of watered-down or un-salty faith have you seen or heard of?

Carefully fill the rest of your cup with water. As the saltiness gets watered down, your egg should sink.

(When you're done, pour your salted water out in a nearby sink, then carefully wipe off your egg and return it to the carton.)

JESUS-FREE FAITH STATION 2: Cleansed By Fire

With your partner, completely cover one side of a tarnished penny with hot sauce and then set it aside for about five minutes. Next, grab another penny and take turns trying to clean it using water, soap, and a rag. Do your very best to clean off that tarnish and make it look totally brand-new.

As you clean your penny, read the following and talk about it:

Some people think they can just polish themselves up to clean away the stain of their sins. Other people think that if they just scrub hard enough by working really hard to live a good life or make up for past mistakes, they can make themselves shiny and new.

•   How have you seen this type of mentality in other people's lives?

•   Do you know any friends who are trying to "clean" or "save" themselves? Why do you think they live that way?

Once five minutes are up, wipe the hot sauce off your penny—it will look much brighter and cleaner than the one you've been trying to clean yourself. Like the hot-sauce penny, *only* the cleansing forgiveness that Jesus offers can truly make us new.

•   Imagine how your friend would feel if he or she believed in Jesus for true forgiveness. What difference would it make in his or her life?

JESUS-FREE FAITH STATION 3: Nice Try

Stand at the starting line and grab a cotton ball, then try to throw it as far as you can. Which mark on the floor did you get to? Try two more times, attempting to beat your previous distance each time.

Now see that candy prize at the end of the lines? If you can throw your cotton ball that far (without changing it in anyway), you can get that prize. Give it a try!

OK, OK, that's sort of a dirty trick…because it is impossible to throw a plain old cotton ball that far. Talk about these questions with your partner:

- Which of you threw your cotton ball farther?

- How far were you from the finish line?

- Lots of people try to get to God by their own efforts. What are some examples of things people try to do to get to God?

Some people may live legitimately "better" lives than others…but no human effort can reach God on its own. Jesus himself said, "No one can come to the Father except through me" (John 14:6b). It's pointless to try to get to God without Jesus.

Study 3

WILL THE REAL GOD PLEASE STAND UP?

Why all roads don't go to the same destination.

Isaiah 45:18; John 14:6; and 1 John 4:1–3

The Lesson at a Glance

Study Sequence	Minutes	What Teenagers Will Do	Supplies
Warm-Up	10 to 15	**Help Yourself Religion and the Belief Buffet**—Create their own religions using some of the major beliefs of pop spirituality.	Photocopies of the "Help Yourself Religion and the Belief Buffet" handout (p. 64), pens, paper, bowl, 7 small snacks (3 healthy, 4 unhealthy), dry-erase board or flip-chart and marker
Investigating the Evidence	10 to 15	**Tasting the Sweetness**—Check out some of the central beliefs of pop spirituality.	Dry-erase board or flip-chart and marker
Bible Focus	20 to 25	**Popping the Bubble**—Compare the beliefs of pop spirituality to Scripture.	Bibles, "The Full Menu" handouts (pp. 65-67), pens, Bible study tools
Life Application	up to 10	**Sharing the Truth With the Hungry**—Consider the type of attitude you need to share Christ with those who get their religion from the belief buffet.	Healthy snacks, dry-erase board or flip-chart and marker

Before the Study

Warm-Up:

* Make photocopies of the **"Help Yourself Religion and the Belief Buffet"** handout (p. 64), and cut them into seven slips each. On the back of each slip, write a number corresponding to the number of the belief on the front of the slip (1 for belief #1 and so on). You'll need enough so there's one slip for every student.

* Set up a "buffet" table with seven snacks—three healthy types of snacks (like raisins, peanuts, or carrot sticks) and four relatively unhealthy types of snacks (like fried potato chips, Twinkies snack cakes, M&M's candies, or packaged cookies). Set all the slips of one number face down in front of a snack, so you have seven piles of numbered slips in front of seven snacks. If the number of participants you have is not divisible by seven, you'll need to make more slips for some of the numbers—just try to make the groups as equal as possible. If you have fewer than seven, just create as many numbered slips as you have participants. Make sure the number of snacks you have corresponds to the number of slips. For example, if snack #1 is carrot sticks and you have three #1 slips, you should have three carrot sticks.

 Bible Focus:
Make photocopies of "The Full Menu" handouts (pp. 65-67) for everyone to have one. Gather pens for everybody and enough Bibles and Bible study tools like Bible dictionaries and concordances so that all of the seven numbered groups have a couple.

Life Application:

* Prepare some healthy snacks such as light popcorn, fruit slices, and cups of juice.

Leader Insight

One of the most popular metaphors about religion that a student in high school or going on to college is likely to hear today is the mountain metaphor. Religion is like a mountain, huge and dark and mysterious inside. And all the different religions are like different roads leading up the mountain to the top. They all have different starting points and they all take different paths, but they're all going to the same destination. Arguing about which road is the best is simply silly, and claiming that yours is the only real road is just pride.

This is the new age of pop spirituality, where all roads lead to heaven and the only real "sin" is claiming to have the exclusive truth. This brand of pop spirituality comes in a variety of packages: from established eastern religious groups to personal meditative practices, from occult rituals to a general belief in reincarnation, from reinvented Jesuses to newly discovered gospels. Beliefs considered exotic or bizarre 20 years ago have carved their way into the West's mind-set. They have gone so far as to become an ordinary part of many people's beliefs, and they are directly opposed to orthodox Christianity.

The trickiest thing about the pop spirituality movement is that it is so hard to define. There isn't any central leader or list of official beliefs. There isn't any accepted name for the groups that make it up. At one point we called it the New Age movement, and many people still use that name today. But the movement has gone beyond the associations with crystals and mediums and astrology. It's made its way into the respectable halls of our major religions, even Christianity, sometimes without people even realizing it. Many Christians have fallen under the influence of what some people are calling "postmodern" spirituality without even realizing that they've jettisoned their Christian beliefs for a mishmash of Eastern mysticism and pop psychology. And that is why it's so important to teach your group to recognize it and refute it when they encounter it.

Even in its new clothes, the pop spirituality movement still contains the same basic set of beliefs that the New Age movement has been pushing for some time. These beliefs are taken from a variety of sources. They bring together everything from Eastern religions (like Hinduism) to Christianity to psychology to environmental issues. Even though many of the beliefs seem contradictory, they all come together under the same banner that was championed by the New Age movement. Essentially, these beliefs are: everything is part of God (or "energy" or "the universe"), sin doesn't exist, and there is no one right religion. In this study you'll examine other beliefs common to the New Age movement and pop spirituality, but these are the three most important.

Remember, the pop spirituality movement is not an ideology that your teenagers *might* encounter; it is a movement that they have *already* encountered—and many have unknowingly been shaped by it. In leading this study, you will be called upon to provide clarity and compassion, helping your group to see through the empty beliefs of the pop spirituality movement to the truth of Christ.

> **tip** Interested in learning more about how a pop spirituality religion like the New Age movement compares to Christianity? Check out the Basic Beliefs Charts and the For Further Research suggestions on pages 136-145!

Warm-Up

⸙ Help Yourself Religion and the Belief Buffet

When teenagers arrive, direct them to help themselves to one snack and to also take one of the numbered slips sitting in front of the snack they chose.

After everyone has gotten their snacks, explain that they should form small groups with other teenagers who have the same number and same snack.

Explain that each small group has been assigned a religious belief and their job is to quickly make up a religion that's centered around the belief that is written on its card. Tell them to eat the snack that goes with their belief while they work on their religion. Here are some questions you should write down on your dry-erase board or flip-chart for small groups to answer while they make up their religions:

- What is the name of your religion? Why?

- What are some other core beliefs that your religion believes are true?

- What is one "holy day" that you have and how does your religion celebrate it?

- Why should someone become a part of your religion?

As you dismiss teenagers to develop their religions, be sure to encourage them to be as creative as possible. Make yourself available to answer any questions teenagers may have about the beliefs on their cards.

After five to 10 minutes, have a spokesperson from each "religion" share the group's answers to the above questions. Follow up the time of sharing by asking the following questions:

- What did you like about being able to make up your own religion?

- Would you follow any of the religions that you've heard about here? Why or why not?

- What are the dangers of making up your own religion?

Prompt teenagers to think for a moment about the snacks they ate at the beginning.

Ask:

- Which groups had the best snacks? Explain.

- If you were to pick some of those snacks to serve at a party, what would you pick? Why?

- If you were training to run in a marathon, which of those snacks would you choose to be part of your diet? Why?

- What would it be like if you had to live off one of these snacks for *all* of your nutrition? How would it affect your body?

- How is eating unhealthy snacks similar to believing in a made-up religion?

Challenge the group to consider that although unhealthy snacks are appealing and taste good, they don't really satisfy the body's nutritional needs. In fact, some of them can be very bad for you.

It would be impossible for a person to live a long and healthy life if his or her entire diet were made up of processed snack foods. Only by eating the "real thing"—truly healthy foods—can a person's physical needs be met.

SAY:

Whether we realize it or not, what we just did when we made up our own religions is very much like what a lot of people do when it comes to choosing their religion. Each of the core beliefs your groups had are core beliefs of the New Age movement, which is the parent of a whole new wave of ideas out there right now that offer all the sweetest parts of spirituality, like salvation and peace and meaning, without all the hard parts like sin and truth and personal responsibility. People are often attracted to these beliefs for the same reason that people are attracted to unhealthy snacks—they are very appealing and offer answers to the spiritual hunger people feel. However, like unhealthy snacks, their ideas can't truly meet the spiritual needs people have. Let's talk more about what these beliefs are and why people find them attractive.

Investigating the Evidence

Tasting the Sweetness

SAY:

One of the trickiest things about the pop spirituality movement is that it is so hard to define. There isn't any central leader or list of official beliefs. There isn't any accepted name for the groups that make it up. It came out of the New Age movement, but it has made its way into every major religion, even Christianity, sometimes without people even realizing it.

Share with them that the pop spirituality movement centers around three main beliefs:

—Everything is part of God.

—Sin doesn't exist.

—There is no one right religion.

Write these three beliefs on your dry-erase board or flip-chart where everyone can see them.

Explain the following central beliefs:

SAY:

The belief that everything is part of "god" is also called pantheism.

Ask:

* Have you heard this belief, or one like it, before? Where?

* What sounds attractive about being part of "god"?

* Is there any truth to this idea?

Explain that pantheism is the belief that god is all. All of reality, everything we see and sense is made up of god. God is not a person but an impersonal force that includes everything and everyone. Popularized on shows like Oprah, this idea of everyone being part of "god" can also be disguised with vague phrases like "the universe" or "energy." This may sound a bit like *Star Wars*—in fact, some versions of pop spirituality are *a lot* like *Star Wars!* People can say that they are part of "god" because they are part of the universal force. You might have heard people say that "god" is an idea that is inside all of us. This is the same basic idea as pantheism.

SAY:

The belief that there is no such thing as sin is one of the main attractions for people who buy into these ideas.

Ask:

- What sounds attractive about the idea that there's no such thing as sin?

- Can you think of any possible downsides to this belief?

- How would you act if you didn't think there were such a thing as sin?

Explain that, instead of salvation from sin, pop spirituality teaches that what we really need is some form of enlightenment. According to them, we need to realize that it's our idea of sin that is holding us back, or we need to experience personal transformation, or we need to realize the divine nature that is already within us. In other words, deep down we're all wonderful—we just need to truly realize it.

The belief that there is no one right religion is one of the most popular in America today and it comes from a meeting between two big ideas. The Eastern tradition of mysticism says that spirituality is too big and mysterious for any one religion to describe it correctly, and the Western philosophy of relativism says that there isn't any real exclusive truth about anything.

Ask:

- Can you think of anywhere that you've heard this belief before? Where?

- Why do you think people are attracted to this idea?

- Do you think it's possible for all religions to be true?

Explain that according to this belief system, religion is like a mountain, all huge and dark and mysterious inside. And all the different religions are like different roads leading up the mountain to the top. They all have different starting points and they all take different paths, but they're all going to the same destination: God. So arguing about which road is the best is silly, and claiming that yours is the only real road is being proud and closed-minded.

Ask:

- Have you ever had someone accuse you of being closed-minded, or been afraid that they would? When?

- Are there any problems you can see with this belief? How would it change your faith and way of living if you believed it?

Some teenagers in your group might actually find it hard to get past the mountain analogy. Don't be afraid if it raises serious doubts in your teenagers' minds. Remind them that you're going to be tackling all of these false beliefs in the Bible Focus section of the study. While they're discussing this false belief, you can always help the discussion along by pointing out that the problem with the mountain analogy is that it assumes that all religions are mankind's made-up ways of approaching spiritual truth. But the Bible is God's way of reaching down to us. We didn't make it—*he* did.

SAY:

The truth is, all of these beliefs, no matter where you see them, are just new clothes on the same basic set of beliefs that the New Age movement has been pushing for some time. These beliefs were taken from a variety of sources. They bring together everything from Eastern religions (like Hinduism) to Christianity to psychology to quantum physics! Even though many of the beliefs seem to contradict each other, they all come together under the same banner of popular "spirituality."

Invite a volunteer to read aloud 1 John 4:1-3.

SAY:

As Christians we need to be able to recognize these beliefs if we're going to preserve and defend our faith against them. Even when they're taught by popular cultural heroes, we need to be able to recognize them for what they are—distortions of the truth. And the very best way we can defend ourselves is by knowing what the Bible has to say about them. Let's find out what the Bible has to say so we don't find ourselves slipping into pop spirituality.

 **Bible Focus**

Popping the Bubble

Even though the influence of the New Age movement is broad, there are some big problems with its beliefs.

Give each person a copy of the **"The Full Menu"** handouts (pp. 65-67). Review the left-hand side of the handout with the group, which describes various core beliefs of the New Age movement and has quotes from New Age or pop spirituality authors.

Have everyone get back into the seven groups they had for the Warm-Up activity, making sure that each group has a Bible, a pen or pencil, and a Bible study tool such as a concordance or Bible dictionary. Ask each group to investigate the belief that it used to create its own made-up religion to see what the Bible has to say about that belief. Teenagers should start with the Scriptures listed on the handout and then use their Bible study tools to find more Scripture passages that apply. Encourage everyone to wrestle with the issues and discover for themselves what the Bible has to say about each area. Let groups know they'll have about 15 minutes to work together, and encourage them to ask for help if they have any questions.

> **tip** If participants haven't used Bible study tools before, such as a concordance or Bible dictionary, be sure to give a quick explanation of how they can best navigate them to find helpful information.

After about 15 minutes, pull the groups back together, and have each group share with the others what it discovered about the belief they were assigned versus what the Bible had to say about it. As the group leader, you will need to help facilitate the discussion by asking clarifying questions such as:

- What would you say to a person who said that particular belief was true?

- What are some verses you know of that could answer that person?

- Why might someone think that that belief was true?

After the sharing time, ask the following questions of the entire group:

- What makes the pop spirituality movement

- dangerous? Explain.

- In your opinion, does Christianity make more sense than pop spirituality? Why or why not? How might you explain your view to a skeptical friend?

Life Application

 Sharing the Truth With the Hungry

Provide some healthy snacks (such as light popcorn, fruit slices, and cups of juice), and invite teenagers to munch on them during this last portion of the lesson.

SAY:

One vital truth to keep in mind is this: People who are involved in pop spirituality or the New Age movement are spiritually hungry. They are honestly dissatisfied with where they are and with what they are experiencing in life. They are hungry for answers. They are looking for *truth*. This is where we come in as believers in Jesus Christ. All the answers to the questions are in Christ. Christianity holds the key to the truth that they desire. Our calling, as followers of Jesus, is to openly and actively share the amazing love and grace of a God who created the spiritual thirst that they feel.

Ask:

- What kind of attitude should we have toward people who are involved in pop spirituality? Explain.

Have teenagers form pairs and challenge them to read Ephesians 4:2, 15; Philippians 2:3; and Colossians 3:12 together. Lead pairs in discussing these questions, allowing time for them to talk after each one:

- What do these verses have to say about our attitude in sharing the truth of Jesus Christ with others? Explain.

- What actions can we take to share the love of Christ with people who believe in pop spirituality?

- What questions could you ask someone who believes in pop spirituality that would lead to a deeper conversation about Jesus?

Invite everyone to gather back together and invite teenagers to share their answers to this last question. As they do, write their ideas on a dry-erase board or flip-chart. If needed, add some of the following questions to their list:

- What or who is God?

- How does God fit into your life?

- What is heaven to you? How do you get there?

- Why do you believe what you believe?

Invite a student to read 2 Peter 3:9.

 SAY:

This verse reminds us about God's heart for those who don't know him. It tells us that God cares about all people. No matter what they've chosen to believe, everyone is still important to God.

Ask:

- What are some words that come to mind when you think about how God feels about those caught up in pop spirituality? Explain.

Conclude by reminding the group that people caught up in pop spirituality are seeking to satisfy the spiritual hunger that all people experience. Our job is simply to show them, out of love, that only the truth and only Christ can fill that hunger. Arguing with others often drives people away from Christianity, while showing love, humility, and genuine concern is usually more effective. It is those attitudes, founded on the truth of Christianity, that God can use to penetrate and change lives.

Encourage your group by reminding them that these conversations may not always be easy, but developing an open dialogue with someone is a great way to show the love of Jesus. If they want it to be productive, though, they're going to need to know their side of it; they need to know what the Bible says in order to be able to share the truth with others. Encourage them to look back through the verses they studied today so they'll always be ready to recognize and respond to the false beliefs of pop spirituality.

Close your time together in prayer, praying specifically for those caught up in the seductive beliefs of pop spirituality. Lead by example by praying for God to give you a loving attitude toward these people and for him to write the truths you've studied on your heart so you can always be ready to offer real, heavenly food to those who are spiritually hungry.

HELP YOURSELF RELIGION AND THE BELIEF BUFFET

Instructions: Photocopy this page and cut it into seven slips.

BELIEF #1

Everything we see, touch, and sense is god.
Everything in the universe is god. God is an impersonal force.

BELIEF #2

All of us are part of god, including you and me.

BELIEF #3

There is no such thing as the problem of sin. The real problem is that we don't understand who we are, our true nature—that we are divine.

BELIEF #4

Salvation is not found in forgiveness of sin, but rather is found in becoming enlightened, experiencing personal transformation, or embracing the fact that the divine already lives in us.

BELIEF #5

You and I will keep coming back in new lives until we are perfect (reincarnation).

BELIEF #6

Jesus is coming back, but it will be as a mass coming. It will be the manifestation of a Christ-consciousness in humanity.

BELIEF #7

There are many sources of "truth"—including the leaders of all the world religions and even you and me. All the world religions worship the same god, just with different names.

The Full Menu

Belief	Quotes	Scriptures
Belief #1: Everything we see, touch, and sense is god. Everything in the universe is god. God is an impersonal force.	*The Aquarian Gospel of Jesus the Christ* states that Jesus said the following: "With much delight I speak to you concerning life—the brotherhood of life. The universal God is one, yet he is more than one; all things are God; all things are one."	• Isaiah 45:18 • Jeremiah 29:11 • Acts 17:31 • 1 Timothy 4:10 • • • Notes:
Belief #2: All of us are part of god, including you and me.	George Trevelyan in *Operation Redemption* commented that every human being is "an eternal droplet of the Divine Ocean, and that potentially it can evolve into a being who can be a co-creator with God." "We are all one." —one of the four messages of God to man in Neale Walsch's *Conversations With God*	• Genesis 1:26-27 • Psalm 95:6-7 • Acts 12:21-23 • • • Notes:
Belief #3: There is no such thing as the problem of sin. The real problem is that we don't understand who we are, our true nature—that we are divine.	"We are all manifestations of Buddha consciousness, of Christ consciousness, only we don't know it." —Joseph Campbell in *The Power of Myth* *The Aquarian Gospel of Jesus the Christ* quotes Jesus as saying, "What I can do all men can do. Go preach the gospel of the omnipotence of Man." "There's nothing we have to do." —one of the four messages of God to man in Neale Walsch's *Conversations With God*	• Psalm 51:5 • Jeremiah 17:9 • Ephesians 2:1-10; 4:18 • 1 John 1:8-9 • • • Notes:

Belief	Quotes	Scriptures
Belief #4: Salvation is not found in forgiveness of sin, but rather is found in being enlightened, experiencing personal transformation, or embracing the fact that the divine already lives in us.	A goal of the New Age movement is to "awaken to the god who sleeps at the root of the human being." —Theodore Roszak in *Unfinished Animal* Madame Blavatsky states, "It is owing to this law of spiritual development that mankind will become freed from its false gods and find itself finally—self-redeemed." —Mark Albrecht in *Reincarnation: A Christian Appraisal*	• John 3:16; 8:12 • Ephesians 2:8-10 • 1 John 5:11-13 • • • Notes:
Belief #5: You and I will keep coming back in new lives until we are perfect (reincarnation).	"Reincarnation is like show business. You just keep doing it until you get it right." —Shirley MacLaine in *Out on a Limb*	• Matthew 25:31-46 • Hebrews 9:24-28; 10:14 • • • Notes:
Belief #6: Jesus is coming back, but it will be as a mass coming. It will be the manifestation of a Christ-consciousness in humanity.	"The second coming of Christ in our age will be fundamentally, most importantly, a mass coming. It will be the manifestation of a consciousness within the multitudes." —David Spangler in *Towards a Planetary Vision* "The Second Coming is occurring now in the hearts and minds of millions of individuals of all faiths as they come to realize this spiritual presence within themselves and each other." — *David Spangler in Cooperation*	• Zechariah 9:14; 12:10 • Matthew 16:27-28; 24:29-30 • Revelation 1:7 • • • Notes:

Belief	Quotes	Scriptures
Belief #7: There are many sources of truth—including the leaders of all the world religions, even you and me. All the world religions worship the same god, just with different names.	*The Aquarian Gospel of Jesus the Christ* quotes Jesus as saying, "The nations of the earth see God from different points of view, and so he does not seem the same to everyone…You Brahmans call him Parabrahm; in Egypt he is Thoth; and Zeus is his name in Greece; Jehovah is his Hebrew name." "Ours is not a better way, ours is merely another way." —one of the four messages of God to man in Neale Walsch's *Conversations with God* "One of the biggest mistakes humans make is to believe there is only one way. Actually, there are many diverse paths leading to what you call God." —Oprah	• Isaiah 44: • Matthew 24:4-5 • John 14:6 • Acts 4:12 • • • Notes:

INHERITED SALVATION

Why no one can be born saved.

Romans 3:22-23; Matthew 22:1-14; and Galatians 3:26-29

The Lesson at a Glance

Study Sequence	Minutes	What Teenagers Will Do	Supplies
Warm-Up	up to 10	**A Place of Honor—** Experience the problem of privilege by receiving (or being denied) special snacks and seats.	Bowl, slips of paper, lots of snacks and drinks, special chairs and tables (or TV trays)
Investigating the Evidence	10 to 15	**Born Lucky—** Explore the ups and downs of the idea of spiritual privilege.	Bibles, photocopies of the "**Born Lucky**" handouts (pp. 83-85)
Bible Focus	15 to 20	**In By the Back Door—** Learn what the Bible has to say about who are God's real chosen people.	Bibles, photocopies of the "**Born Lucky**" handouts (pp. 83-85), dry-erase board or flip-chart
Life Application	10 to 15	**What Would You Say?—** Do a tower-building activity to remind your teenagers of their need for Jesus.	Index cards, measuring tape, several rolls of masking tape, a heavy paperweight or stone, pens

Before the Study

Warm-Up:

*   Prepare slips of paper in this way: about two-thirds of the slips should be blank and the remaining one-third should have a star drawn on them. You'll need one slip for every teenager at the study. Fold up the slips of paper and put them all in a bowl. Also set out two different snack tables. At one, put some great food and drinks like candy, pizza, popcorn, and various soft drinks. Be sure to have lots of food here—enough for all the teenagers in your group. At the other table, put out one simple snack like popcorn or something boring like carrot sticks; also set out cups of water. In addition, change the configuration of your room a bit by creating a "special" seating area, such as a table with nice chairs or even comfy recliners and couches with TV trays.

Investigating the Evidence

*   Make photocopies of the **"Born Lucky"** handouts (pp. 83-85) for everybody to have one.

 Bible Focus:
    Make sure you have enough Bibles for everyone. Also, write the following questions on a dry-erase board or flip-chart where everyone can see them:

*   What happened to the people who were counting on their special place with God in these stories?

*   Why did they lose their place?

*   What qualities is God looking for in his people?

- What kind of people is God definitely not looking for?

- Look at the belief systems on your handout. How do these verses contradict their ideas about spiritual privilege?

- Is there anything else you noticed in your passages that stood out to you?

Life Application:

- You'll need lots of index cards and several rolls of tape for this activity: at least five cards for every student and a roll of tape for every three participants. You'll also need a heavy, nonbreakable paperweight (you can use a rock or a hand weight if you can't find one), one that isn't too large but that is *definitely* heavy enough to crush a tower made out of cards and tape.

- Tape a piece of paper on the weight that labels it "sin." You also need pens or pencils for everyone.

Leader Insight

One of the most obvious questions Christians ask each other when they're getting to know one another is: "How long have you been a Christian?" And almost all of us have heard this answer sometime, from someone: "Oh, I was born a Christian" or "I've always been a Christian." Your teenagers are likely to have heard this answer from their peers. The truth is, lots of people out there believe that they're just born into their faith.

Many young people who believe this are simply confused. They may have grown up in a Christian home, so they don't really know what it means *not* to be Christian. But the Bible clearly tells us that you can't be born into salvation. That's the whole point of the "new birth" that Jesus promised us. We need a new birth because our natural state is sinful.

Lots of people like to believe that they get to start higher up on the totem pole than other people. This is the idea of spiritual privilege: That because of something special about me I get a leg up on the ladder of salvation and holiness. This is clearly against what the Bible teaches. The Bible teaches that all people fall short of the glory of God, and we're all admitted on the same terms to salvation.

The idea of spiritual privilege is one of the most dangerous false teachings your teenagers will encounter. It's dangerous because it makes people complacent and feeds their spiritual pride.
It keeps them from seeing their need for Jesus by telling them that it's enough that they were born into a Christian home, or it's enough that they're part of a certain people group, or that they don't need to strive for holiness because they're part of a special denomination.

God hates the pride of spiritual privilege. As the Bible clearly teaches, salvation can only come from a personal choice to put one's faith in Jesus and holiness can only come from striving to follow God's will and relying on the power of the Holy Spirit. In today's study, you're going to look at what the Bible says about salvation and help your group to dispel the myth of spiritual privilege.

tip Interested in learning more about how Judaism and Hinduism compare to Christianity? Check out the Basic Beliefs Charts and the For Further Research suggestions on pages 136-145!

◊ A Place of Honor

As teenagers arrive, have them each pull a slip of paper from the bowl. When everyone has arrived, tell the group that you're going to start the study with some snacks. Explain that all the people with a star get to select their snacks from the special table and can sit in the special seating area to eat. Let the group know that everyone else gets to eat from the other (boring!) snack table and must find a seat on the floor.

Teenagers will likely complain about this—and rightly so! Allow time for everyone to eat, hang out, and grumble a bit.

Then ask everybody:

*   For those of you given the special food and seats, what does it feel like to be in a privileged position?

*   Everybody else—what do you think about this situation? How do you feel about me and my rules right now? How do you feel about the privileged people?

*   Imagine your life was really like this—you really did have special privileges over everybody else, or you were denied privileges others got. How would that affect you in the long run?

It's hard, isn't it, dealing with people who think they should have a special place ahead of others.

Let the group know that the social "experiment" is over and now everybody—star or no star—can get snacks from the good table and can sit wherever they want. Once everyone is settled again, ask the group:

- What situations can you think of in life in which you've seen some people get a privileged position over others?

SAY:

Some people live as if they've got special spiritual privileges. They think that because of who they are they're in a special position with God. They think you can be born into salvation. Or at least they think that they're born holier than the next guy and should be given a leg up. Let's take a look now at some of these groups that think they were "born lucky."

Investigating the Evidence

Born Lucky

Give everybody a copy of the **"Born Lucky"** handouts (pp. 83-85).

SAY:

Each of the religious traditions on this handout represent groups of people who think they've been given the keys to the front door of heaven for one reason or another. The truth is, lots of people out there believe that who they are gives them some special spiritual status.

Have teenagers form small groups of three to five. Assign each small group to one of the five belief systems listed on the handout. Tell the groups to read through their topic and discuss the questions listed after it. Give the small groups about five minutes to read and discuss, then bring everyone back together. Have each small group give a brief explanation of their assigned belief system and what they think the problems are with those beliefs, based on their discussion of the follow-up questions.

After all the small groups have shared, **ask:**

*   Why do you think people find these kinds of teachings attractive?

SAY:

Lots of people like to believe that they get to start higher up on the totem pole than other people. This is the idea of spiritual privilege: That because of something special about me I get a leg up on the ladder of salvation and holiness.

Ask:

- What are the possible dangers of thinking that you have spiritual privilege?

SAY:

The idea of spiritual privilege is one of the most dangerous false teachings you'll encounter. It can even be common among Christians. For example, you may have heard people say "I was born a Christian" or "I have always been a Christian." Sometimes people who think this way are confused about what it really means to be saved. They're unable to really see their need for Jesus because they think it's simply enough that they were born into a Christian home. Or perhaps you've heard people talk more about their denomination than they ever talk about Jesus—they may feel that they don't need to strive for holiness because they're part of a special denomination that they feel is "better" than all the others.

Explain to your group that this is clearly against what the Bible teaches. Have them look up John 3:3-5 and Romans 3:22-23.

Ask:

- How do these verses conflict with the idea of spiritual privilege?

Explain that if we could be born saved, we wouldn't need a new birth; we need a new birth because our natural state is sinful.

SAY:

Now that we've had a chance to see some of the problems with the idea of spiritual privilege, let's look at what the Bible has to tell us about who God's chosen people really are.

Tell your group to keep their handouts handy, because they're going to need them for the next activity.

 Bible Focus

In By the Back Door

Have everybody get out their Bibles and return to their groups from the **"Born Lucky"** activity. Explain that each group will be reading a parable—a story Jesus told to illustrate a spiritual truth, then assign at least one of the following Scripture passages to each group. (Make sure each passage is assigned to at least one group.)

- Matthew 21:33-43

- Matthew 22:1-14

- Matthew 25:1-13

- Luke 13:6-9

- Luke 18:9-14

SAY:

Remember, each of the religious traditions on your handout represent groups of people who think they've been given a special key to the front door of heaven. But God is a fan of the back door.

As teenagers read, draw their attention to the following questions that you've written on your dry-erase board or flip-chart:

- What happened to the people who were counting on their special place with God in these stories?

- Why did they lose their place?

- What qualities is God looking for in his people?

- What kind of people is God definitely not looking for?

- Look at the belief systems on your handout. How do these verses contradict their ideas about spiritual privilege?

- Is there anything else you noticed in your passages that stood out to you?

Prompt small groups to talk about their parables, making sure to discuss their answers to the questions you've posted.

Allow five to ten minutes for discussion, then have everybody gather back together and invite a volunteer from each small group to share what "back-door" qualities God is looking for, based on their group's discussion.

Ask everyone to look up Galatians 3:26-29 and invite a volunteer to read it aloud.

SAY:

God hates the pride of spiritual privilege. As the Bible clearly teaches, salvation can only come from a personal choice to put your faith in Jesus, and holiness can only come from striving to follow him through the power of the Holy Spirit within us. Now let's do an activity to help remind us of our need for Christ.

Life Application

 What Would You Say?

Have everybody form new groups of three or four and give each group a stack of at least 15 index cards and pens or pencils. In their groups, have teenagers write on each card something special about themselves or something they've accomplished that some people would consider to be spiritually impressive. Here are some examples: "I've been a member of my church for 10 years," "My grandfather was a pastor," "I read the Bible every day and pray every night," "Everyone in my family is saved," "I've been baptized," "I've never broken the law," "I've memorized an entire book of the Bible," "I regularly do charity work," or "I'm a (name of your church or denomination)."

(If some teenagers have no idea what to write about themselves, suggest that they make up some claims of spiritual privilege—things that others might say.)

When they are done, **SAY:**
Now you need to build a tower using your cards and tape. Try to make it as tall as you can and as sturdy as you can. Your goal is to build a tower as tall as I am, if you can.

Give groups tape, and let them go at it. When the towers are complete, **SAY:**
Now let's see how high you managed to build your towers.

Take some measuring tape and measure to see how tall trios managed to get their towers. Congratulate them on their accomplishments.

Ask:

- Have you ever known or heard of somebody—in real life or on TV—who lives like this? Who tries to prop himself or herself up by their spiritual accomplishments? Without sharing names, what's that person like?

- Why do you think they think that way?

SAY:

Now let's see how well you've built your towers.

Take your paperweight that you labeled "sin" and explain to the group that because none of us are perfect, not only does our tower of accomplishments need to lift us up, but it also has to hold up the weight of all our mistakes that weigh us down.

One at a time, let a volunteer from each small group place the "sin" weight on their tower and see what happens. (Predictably, they will not be able to hold up the weight.)

Ask:

- Why didn't our towers hold up?

- Whose standard do you think would actually be harder to reach: God's standard or the standard I set for you in this activity? Why?

Remind teenagers that nothing they do and nothing about who they are is enough to bring them even remotely closer to God's standard. Only Christ can do that because only Christ can take away the weight of our sins and lift us up with him.

Give teenagers paper and pencils or pens.

Now I'd like you to think about what you might say to someone who believes in spiritual privilege. How might you use what you know about his or her faith and your own faith to help that person see the need for Jesus? Try to begin with what you would agree on and then work toward the uniqueness of faith in Jesus.

Give teenagers several minutes to take notes on their thoughts, then allow volunteers to share what they might say. Keep going until several have shared, and make sure to affirm their ideas.

Wrap up this study by having teenagers form pairs and discuss the following questions with their partners:

- How has this study reminded you of your own need for Jesus?

- How has it changed or reinforced your own view of your spiritual standing?

Close your time together by having pairs pray with each other. Encourage them to pray for people who are blinded by their belief in their position of spiritual privilege. Also, suggest that they pray about their own reliance upon Jesus for salvation.

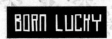

BORN LUCKY

Hinduism:

Hindus believe in a system called the caste system. The caste system arranges people into four classes: priests, nobles, peasants, and manual laborers. People outside the caste system are outcasts (or "untouchables") who are considered to be lower than most animals. People born into the higher castes are spiritually privileged, and are believed to be born into their caste because they're better people who lived better previous lives. People born into a lower caste are simply getting what they deserve.

Hindus also believe in Dharma: if something has always been a certain way, it should continue to be that way. Since each person's lot in life is due to his or her actions in a previous life, each person should be content with his or her position in life. To try and move out of one's caste or class in a person's lifetime is considered a sin.

- Given these beliefs, what do you think a person of a high religious caste would do if he passed someone from a lower caste or an outcast injured on the road (like in the tale of the Good Samaritan in the Bible)?

- How does this make you feel?

- Step into the shoes of someone else and imagine how you would feel if you were born an outcast—an "untouchable." What would you think about God (or the gods of Hinduism)? What would you think of yourself?

Judaism:

Jews are part of a racial and religious group that believes they were chosen specially by God to be his people. The Old Testament describes in detail how God chose the Jewish people to be *his*—to have a special role of pointing all other people groups to him. Jews today do not actively seek to convert other people to Judaism. They believe that their relationship with God as his people is something special that belongs to them by birth. After Christ's resurrection, one of the big hurdles that even the disciples had a hard time accepting was the idea that God would offer even non-Jews (Gentiles) the chance to become a part of his people. This belief in their privilege is still maintained by modern Jews today.

- How would it make you feel if you asked someone if you could join God's people and his answer was, "Why? You're not one of us"? Explain.

- Would you be very likely to want to believe in his God? Why or why not?

Sectarianism:

Many cultures and denominations believe that being a part of their racial group or their denomination gives them a special position with God. Amusing phrases like "If you ain't Dutch, you ain't much" and "God has a special place in heaven for the Scottish" cover over deeply held beliefs by many groups that they have a special spiritual privilege because they're part of a certain people. Many Christian denominations have similar attitudes. They think that only people from their group will go to heaven or that the best spots in heaven will be reserved for their church. Or they might think that just belonging to a certain superior denomination is enough to get them into heaven. They think that their church "membership card" is like a free pass into heaven.

- Have you ever met people with this kind of attitude? Who?

- How did it make you feel?

- Have you ever noticed this type of pride among people in your own church or denomination? How do you think it affects outsiders or Christians from other churches?

Jehovah's Witnesses:

Jehovah's Witnesses believe that only a choice number of people, belonging to their religion, will go to heaven to rule with God. Only 144,000 people will have this privilege. Other faithful but less exalted Jehovah's Witnesses who don't quite make the cut will get to live on a new Earth, and everyone else will be destroyed. So even within the Jehovah's Witnesses you have to be constantly striving to be part of the elite spiritual club that gets the better afterlife.

* How do you think it would it make you feel if you believed that only a privileged few got to rule with God in heaven?

* How would it change your view of God?

Mormonism:

Mormons believe that faithful Mormon men will be exalted and become gods. Women can only be exalted if they're sealed in marriage to a Mormon man. It's nice if you're a man, but half of the human population isn't so lucky unless they're willing to get hitched!

* If you're a girl, how does this belief make you feel? If you're a guy, does this belief sound fair to you? Explain.

* How does this belief conflict with what you believe personally or what you know from the Bible?

Study 5

ALL GOD'S CHILDREN

Why believing in God just isn't enough.

Hebrews 8:6-13; Matthew 22:34-40; and 1 John 4:7-12

The Lesson at a Glance

Study Sequence	Minutes	What Teenagers Will Do	Supplies
Warm-Up	**5 to 10**	**A Rose By Any Other Name—** Play a game of mixed-up names and discuss the apparent similarities between Judaism, Islam, and Christianity.	Photocopies of "A Rose By Any Other Name" handout (p. 104), tape, dry-erase board and marker
Investigating the Evidence	**30 to 35**	**The Pillars and the Principles—** Work in pairs to compare Islamic or Jewish religious practices to Christianity, then teach each other what they've learned.	Bibles; "The Pillars and the Principles" handouts (pp. 105-109); numbered signs; child's puzzle-box toy, paper, tape; yellow construction paper; map of the Middle East; several heavy books; several pillows; item of kosher food; cups, sparkling grape juice, matzo bread

...chart continued on pg. 88

The Lesson at a Glance...continued

Study Sequence	Minutes	What Teenagers Will Do	Supplies
Bible Focus 	10 to 15	**The Limits of the Law—** Discuss the different motivations driving Judaism, Islam, and Christianity and why belief in God and the Law isn't enough.	Bibles
Life Application	5 to 10	**The Motivation That Matters—** Challenge teenagers to find ways to live out love in their faith.	Index cards, pens

Before the Study

Warm-Up:

Make several photocopies of the **"A Rose By Any Other Name"** handout (p. 104). You'll need one for yourself and another copy for volunteers to read. Cut both copies into thirds, separating the three "Who Am I?" sections. Tape the three sections from one of the handouts up on your dry-erase board side by side. To the left of them, write these three names on your dry-erase board, one above the other: Maewyn Succat, Maimoni, Hazrat Babajan.

Investigating the Evidence

On one side of the room, hang up five numbered signs (1 through 5) along the wall with space between each. At each station, set out a few copies of the corresponding "Islam" station instructions from **"The Pillars and the Principles"** handouts (pp. 105-109). Also, set out the following:

• Islam Station 1:
  You'll need a plastic or wooden children's puzzle box—the type of toy which has various shaped holes on each side and corresponding wooden or plastic shapes that fit in each hole. Cover every hole of the box with paper and tape, except for one hole. (Make sure the paper covers each section separately so that it will not need to be torn when teenagers open up the puzzle.) Set out all the shapes and label each one with names of religious leaders and great people, like Muhammad, Gandhi, Mother Teresa, and so on. Label the piece that fits the uncovered hole "Jesus." Also, tape a piece of paper inside the puzzle box that says "Only Jesus fits because he and the Father are one."

- Islam Station 2:
  No supplies needed.

- Islam Station 3:
  Set out pens and a bunch of circles cut from yellow construction paper. They will be "coins" and should be about 2 to 3 inches in diameter. You'll want several coins for each pair that will visit this station.

- Islam Station 4:
  No supplies needed.

- Islam Station 5:
  Set out a map that includes Saudi Arabia (and Mecca). Highlight or underline Mecca on the map.

On the other side of the room, hang five numbered signs (1 through 5) along the wall with space in between them. At each station, set out a few copies of the corresponding "Judaism" station instructions from **"The Pillars and the Principles"** handouts (pp. 105-109). Also, set out the following:

- Judaism Station 1:
  Set out several heavy books (like dictionaries or other reference books).

- Judaism Station 2:
  No supplies needed.

- Judaism Station 3:
  Set out several comfortable pillows.

- Judaism Station 4:
  Set out a jar, can, or box of kosher food. Be sure that it has a
  label specifically identifying it as kosher. (Just ask your local
  grocer to direct you to the kosher foods section.)

- Judaism Station 5:
  Set out some small paper or plastic cups, one or more bottles
  of red sparkling grape juice, and a plate of matzo bread,
  broken up into pieces. (You may also want to set a small
  garbage can near this station.)

Life Application:

- Gather enough index cards and pens for all the participants
  to have one of each.

Millions of people today claim to believe in God. According to a 2003 Harris poll, 90% of all American adults believe in God. If you narrowed things down and asked in a poll how many people believed in the God of Abraham, Isaac, and Jacob—a personal God who is infinite, all-powerful, all-knowing, makes himself known in history, punishes sin, and seeks reconciliation with his children—the number would probably drop dramatically.

The truth is, believing in "god" isn't the same thing as believing in God. Even among those religions that are most like Christianity and claim to worship the same God that we do, believing in God isn't the same as trusting in Christ's death on the cross to save us from sin.

Some of these religions, like Islam and Judaism, even look a lot like Christianity. We all pray, we all give money to the poor, we all believe in the God of Abraham, we all believe that God has revealed himself in history to bring us back to him, we all preach the importance of devotion and submission to God, we all believe in similar rules of morality, we all engage in religious practices like fasting, and so on.

> **tip** Mormonism is another religion that is very similar to Christianity. But since this religion, like the Jehovah's Witnesses and Christian Science, claims to be a type of Christianity, it belongs to a group known as cults, which you'll get to study separately in study 6.

"So what's the real difference?" your teenagers might ask. It's not an unusual question. Even one of our presidents once remarked that he believed Muslims and Christians worship the same God. Even if they don't agree that Muslims worship the same God, it's very natural for your teenagers to look at things and think, "Well, it is true that Jews worship the same God; they even have a lot of the same Scriptures. Doesn't that mean they're going to heaven?"

In today's study, you'll examine some of the real similarities and real differences between Christianity and the other faiths that claim the same God. As the leader, it's your mission to help your teenagers understand that even though there may be some truth in these religions, and even though there are some good things about them that we could learn from, looking the same and sounding the same doesn't mean they *are* the same.

Christians have a fundamentally different understanding of God from Jews and Muslims, and because of it we have a fundamentally different motivation behind the way we practice our faith. Christians have the revelation of Jesus Christ, who freely and sacrificially revealed the love of God to us though his death on the cross. That love transforms our understanding of God. And even though our practices may look similar, everything we do is done because of our love for God, who first loved us, not because it's the Law. That change in motivation makes all the difference in the world.

tip Interested in learning more about how Islam and Judaism compare to Christianity? Check out the Basic Beliefs Charts and the For Further Research suggestions on pages 136-145!

Warm-Up

◊ A Rose By Any Other Name

As teenagers arrive, welcome them and take some time to greet them by name.

Then **SAY:**
Shakespeare once wrote a famous quote: "A rose by any other name would smell as sweet." What he meant was it doesn't matter if you call something by different names; it's still what it is. Well, today you get to prove how much you can tell about someone when you take away their names.

Explain that they're going to play a guessing game where they have three mixed-up names they have to match up with three descriptions. Pass out the three sections of the "A Rose By Any Other Name" handout (p. 104) to three volunteers. Invite them to read the descriptions aloud, then give the group some time to discuss which description they think belongs to which of the names written on the dry-erase board. Explain that you can't give them any clues other than what's in the handout.

Once your group has decided which name they think belongs to which description, don't correct them if they've guessed wrong. Then explain to them that there's a second part to the game. The fact is, not all of the people listed are Christians. Some of them might belong to other religions. Write "Christian," "Muslim," and "Jewish" on the dry-erase board and invite the group to also guess which person belongs to which religion. Give everybody a chance to discuss and come up with their guesses and write them down on the board.

Next, share the correct answers with the group:

—Hazrat Babajan (#1) was a famous Muslim saint who spent the last years of her life living under a mahogany tree.

—Maewyn Succat (#2) became a Christian and returned to preach to the people who kidnapped and enslaved him. He is better known as Saint Patrick of Ireland.

—Maimoni (#3), also known as Maimonides or Rambam, was a famous physician and is one of the most respected Jewish rabbis of all time.

Draw lines on the dry-erase board connecting the correct names, descriptions, and religions.

Ask:

• How hard was it to guess the names of the people based on the descriptions you were given?

- How easy or hard was it to guess the religions of the three people based on the descriptions?

The truth is, monotheistic religions like Islam, Judaism, and Christianity have a lot in common. They all believe in the God of Abraham. They all believe in a personal God who is infinite, all-powerful, all-knowing, and perfect. They all believe that this God has spoken through his prophets in order to bring us back to him. They even have very similar religious practices. We all do a lot of the same things, so much that unless you're given certain details, it's hard to tell who belongs to what religion.

The question is, is there really any difference between them? Don't we all worship the same God, after all? And isn't that what's important? In the next part of the lesson, we're going to look at some of the central features of these other religions that believe in God and try to see how they're similar and how they're really different from Christianity.

Investigating the Evidence

The Pillars and the Principles

Have your teenagers number off into two groups. Send all the 1's to one side of your meeting room and all the 2's to the other. Tell everyone to pair up with a partner who's on their side of the room. Once everyone has paired up (and the group is roughly divided in half, on each side of the room), explain what pairs will be doing.

SAY:

All the 1's will be looking at Islam and all the 2's will be exploring Judaism—you'll each compare and contrast what you learn with Christianity.

Both Muslims and Jews believe that in order to go to heaven, they must regularly perform certain religious duties, such as prayer or giving money to the poor or practicing certain rituals. Both religions put a lot of emphasis on submitting your life to God and living your life the way he wants you to.

Explain that Islam prescribes five essential duties in worship, also called the five pillars of Islam. Orthodox Judaism also has key principles for how its members should live their lives. Draw teenagers' attention to the numbered signs on the wall in their half of the room and let them know that each one represents either a pillar of Islam or a key principle of Orthodox Judaism.

Tell the group that pairs will need to go to each numbered station on their side of the room and follow the instructions written there. Let teenagers know that they should carry their Bibles with them to each station. Also, explain that they'll have

20 minutes total, so they should take about four minutes at each station. Let them know that they can go to their assigned stations in any order they'd like.

Once everybody understands what they're supposed to do, have pairs get started. To help pairs keep track of time, warn the group when 10 minutes have passed and again when there are just 5 minutes left.

When about 20 minutes have passed, instruct the pairs to form a small group of four by joining up with a pair from the other side of the room. (In other words, each new group of four should have two teenagers who learned about Islam and two teenagers who learned about Judaism.) Tell small groups to take a few minutes to teach each other about the five key ideas of Islam or Judaism that they looked at. Then have small groups discuss these questions:

- What did you think of Islam or Judaism before you went through these stations? What do you think now? What surprised you? What changed in your opinions?

- What similarities did you see between how Jews and Muslims practice their faith and how Christians practice theirs?

- What do you see as the key differences?

Have everyone gather back together as a small group and review these questions again, inviting teenagers to share what their small groups discussed regarding similarities and differences between Islam, Judaism, and Christianity. Affirm their responses.

Then **SAY:**

Muslims, Jews, and Christians share some very similar spiritual exercises. Followers of all three religions commit themselves to God and rely on him. All of them pray and give their money to those in need. All of them have scriptures that they study to learn more about God and engage in religious practices like fasting.

Muslims and Orthodox Jews perform their spiritual exercises regularly and rigorously. Perhaps Christians should see their devotion as a challenge to be more devoted to God and Christian practice. However, their motivations for devotion have a major difference. Let's look at that now.

---

tip   Don't be surprised if you encounter some relativistic thinking along these lines: "Muslims worship Allah; Christians worship God. Both religions have spiritual practices that in many cases appear more similar than dissimilar. So it doesn't matter how or why we worship, just that we all worship God." It *does* matter. Both Islam and Christianity can't be true. They can appear similar in practice, but they have contradictory theology, as evidenced by the Islamic emphasis on law and the Christian emphasis on love.

 Bible Focus

The Limits of the Law

Ask for volunteers to look up James 2:19 and Matthew 7:21-22 and have them read the verses aloud.

Ask:

- After reading these verses, do you think believing in God, even having the correct idea of God, is enough to be saved? Why or why not?

SAY:

Jesus said that no one comes to the Father except through him. All the other religions, including Islam and even Judaism, couldn't get to God because the way they were using just didn't work. Jesus came to the earth because they didn't work. They tried to understand and approach God through the Law. But the Law was just a shadow of the truth. It looked similar to the thing it was a shadow of, but it wasn't the real thing. That's how it is with the Muslim and Jewish beliefs and practices. They look similar, but they're only shadows of the real thing.

Ask everyone to look up Hebrews 8:6-7 and have a volunteer read it aloud.

SAY:

Earlier, we looked at some essential Jewish and Islamic practices. Essential is the key word because these duties are in no way optional. They follow the laws because the Law is the basis for the Jewish and Muslim ways to salvation.

Ask:

- From what you've read and learned, what was wrong with the old covenant of the Law?

Invite volunteers to read aloud Hebrews 8:8-13, Matthew 22:34-40, and 1 John 4:7-12 while everyone else reads along in their own Bibles.

Ask:

- How would you put the idea of the "new covenant" in your own words? What is it that makes things different between the old covenant and the new one?

SAY:

Christians have the revelation of Jesus Christ, who freely and sacrificially revealed the love of God to us though his death on the cross. That love transforms our understanding of God. And even though our practices may look similar, everything we do is done because of our love for God, who first loved us, not because it's the Law.

Ask:

- If Christianity centers around our love for God and the love of God for us, demonstrated by Jesus, why is it important for Christians to practice things like prayer and church attendance?

Share that out of all the world religions, only Christianity can be summarized by love. Christians don't do things in order to earn salvation—they know they could never do enough on their own strength. Instead, they do what they do in response to the love freely and sacrificially offered by God through Jesus Christ.

Life Application

 The Motivation That Matters

Remind teenagers that although Muslims, Jews, and Christians practice their religions in some similar ways, there is a big difference in their motivation.

SAY:

Since Christians are motivated by the desire to know and love a compassionate and personal God, let's review what we've learned today by coming up with some answers to this question:

- How can Christians effectively show love for God and others through our religious practices?

Give everyone an index card and a pen, then invite teenagers to wander around the room as a way to review some of the Jewish, Islamic, and Christian practices they learned about. Challenge them to zero in on three of the stations or ideas that most interested them and spend some time reflecting on what they learned there. Prompt them to try to come up with (and write down) one specific personal application they can draw from each station. For example, a student could write, "Pray for one minute five times a day" or choose one of the acts of service listed on the coins. Make sure everybody understands that you are not advising them to mimic Muslim or Jewish practices, but instead to practice true Christian devotion to Jesus Christ. Also encourage teenagers to make goals realistic and measurable—like "Record prayer requests and answers weekly" instead of "Pray for five hours each day" or "Pray more."

After a few minutes, ask everybody to choose just *one* of the goals they wrote down to focus on this week. Close in prayer by asking that God would work in your life and the lives of your teenagers to reveal the love of God to others. Remind everyone to take their cards with them, both as reminders for this week's application and also as a challenge to move on to another application point in the future.

A ROSE BY ANY OTHER NAME

#1: WHO AM I?

I was born into royalty, but when I was young I left my home to devote my life to God. I memorized the scriptures at an early age and spent years living in the mountains. I always prayed five times a day. During my life I went on many pilgrimages, and I often gathered food for the poor and tended to other pilgrims who had become sick. I became famous for my acts of piety and kindness and had many devoted followers. I spent the last years of my life living under a mahogany tree, and there is now a memorial over that tree where I died.

#2: WHO AM I?

When I was young I was kidnapped and sold as a slave in another country. After six years, I managed to escape and returned home to my family. Later, though, I went back to the people who had kidnapped me to tell them about God. I made thousands of converts while I was there, including many powerful men and women. At one point I was beaten, robbed, and put in chains. When some of my adopted people were kidnapped and made slaves, I fought for their freedom and to convince the local leaders not to allow slavery.

#3: WHO AM I?

I learned the Scriptures from my father at an early age, but when I was young my home was invaded and my family was forced to leave. For years I wandered the country and learned all I could by reading and listening to the teachings of others. Later, I became a famous physician and even tended to kings. Every day I would work until I was weak and hungry to heal the illnesses of my people. At the same time, I studied the Scriptures closely and wrote many famous works explaining them to the people.

ISLAM
STATION 1: Allah and Muhammad

Read the following quotes:

"Muhammad is not the father of any man among you, but he is the messenger of Allah and the Seal of the Prophets; and Allah is aware of all things" (Koran 33:40).

"There is no god but Allah, and Muhammad is the apostle of Allah."

Now read John 10:27-33.

Discuss this question:

• What similarities or differences do you notice between Muhammad's and Jesus' claims about themselves?

Look at the toy with all the holes covered but one, then find the piece that fits into that hole. Put it inside, then open the toy and read the statement inside. (When you're done, take the piece out and return the toy to the way you found it.)

ISLAM
STATION 2: Prayer

Read the following verses from the Koran:

"In the name of Allah, the Beneficent, the Merciful,
Praise be to Allah, Lord of the Worlds,
The Beneficent, the Merciful.
Owner of the Day of Judgment,
Thee (alone) we worship; Thee (alone) we ask for help.
Show us the straight path,
The path of those whom Thou hast favored;
Not (the path) of those who earn Thine anger nor of those who go astray."

(Koran 1:1-7)

Muslims pray five times a day facing Mecca. This prayer is part of all corporate and private worship.

Now read the Lord's Prayer found in Matthew 6:9-13.

Discuss this question:

• What similarities or differences do you notice between the prayer Muslims are taught to pray and the prayer Jesus taught his followers?

ISLAM

STATION 3: Almsgiving

Read this verse from the Koran:

"The alms are only for the poor and the needy, and those who collect them, and those whose hearts are to be reconciled, and to free the captives and the debtors, and for the cause of Allah, and (for) the wayfarers; a duty imposed by Allah. Allah is Knower, Wise" (Koran 9:60).

Now read Matthew 6:2-4 and 2 Corinthians 9:7.

Discuss this question:

* What similarities or differences do you notice between the two religions' motivation for giving?

As a pair, brainstorm acts of service Christian teenagers might perform (such as giving money to the church or volunteering at a soup kitchen). Grab some paper coins and write down a few of the acts of service you've thought of (one per coin). When you're done, spread your coins down on the ground by your station.

ISLAM

STATION 4: Fasting

Read these verses from the Koran:

"O ye who believe! Fasting is prescribed for you, even as it was prescribed for those before you, that ye may ward off (evil)…Allah desireth for your ease; He desireth not hardship for you; and (He desireth) that ye should [fast during the month of Ramadan], and that ye should magnify Allah for having guided you, and that…ye may be thankful" (Koran 2:183, 185).

Now read Matthew 4:1-4 and 2 Timothy 1:7.

Discuss this question:

* Fasting reminds Muslims to rely on Allah. On what things or what people do you rely on besides God?

ISLAM

STATION 5: Pilgrimage to Mecca

Find Mecca on the map. Now read these quotes:

"Lo! the first Sanctuary appointed for mankind was that at [M]ecca, a blessed place, a guidance to the peoples; Wherein are plain memorials (of Allah's guidance); the place where Abraham stood up to pray; and whosoever entereth it is safe. And pilgrimage to the House is a duty unto Allah for mankind, for him who can find a way thither" (Koran 3:96-97).

"By this annual assembly, Islam is bound together in a visible rite of unity."

Read John 17:20-23 and Hebrews 10:25.

Discuss this question:

*   What similarities or differences do you notice between the Islamic annual pilgrimage to Mecca and Christian weekly church attendance?

JUDAISM

STATION 1: The Commandments

Read Exodus 20:3-17 aloud from your Bible.

It is very important for an Orthodox Jew to follow all of these commandments. It is also expected that they follow every one of the 613 *mitzvot*—365 negative commandments and 248 positive commandments (though some are obsolete now since the destruction of the Temple). These commandments cover almost every area of life, from what you believe to how you cut your hair to how you treat others.

Try to walk across the room and back to this spot while balancing one of the books at this station on your head—without using your hands! As you do, imagine what it would be like to try to live in a way that "holds up" all these laws and commandments at all times.

Talk about these questions:

*   How hard was it to carry the burden of that heavy book on your head without it slipping off?

*   How hard do you think it'd be to try to uphold the Ten Commandments and over 600 other regulations every day of your life?

Read John 13:34 and Matthew 22:36-40.

Discuss this question:

*   What do you think of the list of commandments Jesus gives for Christians? Is it simpler or more complex than the old list?

JUDAISM
STATION 2: Circumcision

Circumcision is an outward sign of the Jewish covenant with God.
All Jewish males are required to be circumcised (the removal of the foreskin from the male), usually as infants. Uncircumcised adult converts to Judaism technically still need to be circumcised! It's so important, in fact, that uncircumcised Jews who die will sometimes be circumcised before burial.

Read Colossians 2:9-12. Also read Romans 2:29, which says, "true circumcision is not merely obeying the letter of the law; rather it is a change of heart produced by God's Spirit."

Discuss this question:

* How is the Christian concept of circumcision of the heart different from the Jewish practice? How is it similar?

JUDAISM
STATION 3: Shabbat

Grab a pillow and lay back on the ground to rest for a moment.

Shabbat is the weekly day of rest (the Sabbath). It commemorates the seventh day of creation, when God rested. There are strict rules about what you can or cannot do for the 24 hours of this period every week. There are 39 different categories of activities you cannot do, including driving, turning electrical devices on or off, tying or untying things, filtering water, and picking bones from fish.

Take some time trying to imagine how you would get through your day without being able to do the things listed above.

Read Mark 2:23-28 and Colossians 2:16-17.

Discuss this question:

* What do you think it means that the *fulfillment* of the Sabbath is found in Christ? What do you think Christians are meant to learn from the Sabbath?

JUDAISM
STATION 4: Kashrut

Kashrut (as in "kosher") refers to the Jewish dietary laws. Jews must only eat kosher foods; they can't eat anything without being certain that it is acceptable according to their rules of what kinds of things and what methods of preparation are correct. No pig products are allowed, no mixing meat with dairy, no processed foods unless they're from a kosher factory, no blood, no gelatin or cheese unless it's specially approved, no eating of animals that died from natural causes, no foods prepared with utensils or machinery that was also used on non-kosher food, and so on. Not only does it matter what foods you eat, it matters what you eat them with, how you store them, when you eat them, who prepared them, and how they were grown. When orthodox Jews shop, they either have to go to a special kosher market or they can only buy items at the supermarket that are specially marked as being kosher.

Read Romans 14:3, 20-21.

Discuss this question:

•   What examples can you think of where your indulgence in something might cause someone else to stumble, even if it's not a problem for you?

JUDAISM
STATION 5: Holidays

Celebrating Jewish holidays is a very important part of Jewish identity. You have probably heard of two very famous Jewish holidays: Passover (Pesach) and Hanukkah. There are many other holidays and observances that set the rhythm for the year in an Orthodox Jewish home, including Rosh Hashanah (the Jewish New Year), Yom Kippur (the Day of Atonement), and Sukkot (the Feast of Booths or Tabernacles).

God himself established the remembrance of holidays as a very important element in the life of his people. During Passover, for example, Jews eat a special meal including matzo bread and wine to remember how God saved his people from the Egyptians. Go ahead and drink some sparkling juice and a piece of matzo bread.

In Exodus 12, God gave his people instructions for how to celebrate the Passover. Read what he said about how important it was in Exodus 12:14, 17, and 24.

Talk about these questions with your partner:

•   Why do you think it was so important to God that his people celebrated this holiday every year?

•   What affect would it have on a person—and his or her faith—to celebrate so many God-focused holidays every year?

Study 6

UNORTHODOXY

Why the secrets of the cults can't compare to true Christianity.

John 1:1-18 and Philippians 2:5-11

The Lesson at a Glance

Study Sequence	Minutes	What Teenagers Will Do	Supplies
Warm-Up	up to 15	**Truth or Lies**—Play a question game where they have to sort out lies from truths.	Index cards, pencils
	5 to 10	**Back to Basics**—Describe some basic orthodox Christian beliefs.	5 large sheets of newsprint or poster board, marker, tape
Investigating the Evidence	15 to 20	**New and Improved!**—Create ads for the cults that explain their differences with Christianity and show why they're attractive.	Construction paper, pieces of poster board, scissors, markers, paper, pencils, and other art supplies
Bible Focus	15 to 20	**Making the Cut**—Examine the challenges of the cults to orthodox Christianity in light of the Bible.	Bibles, pencils, photocopies of **"Comparing the Cults"** handouts (pp. 129-132)

...chart continued on pg. 112

The Lesson at a Glance...continued

Study Sequence	Minutes	What Teenagers Will Do	Supplies
Life Application	**up to 15**	**Diving in Deeper—** Commit to growing as a Confident Christian by studying the truth.	Bills of play money, photocopies of the **"Nicene Creed"** handout (p. 133) or your own church's statement of faith, dry-erase board and markers, photocopies of the **"Confidence Builders"** handouts (pp. 134-135)

Before the Study

Warm-Up:

*   Set out enough pencils and index cards so that everybody gets one. Also, on the top of five separate large sheets of newsprint or poster board, write "God," "Jesus," "the Bible," "humanity," and "sin" and then hang them up where everyone can see them.

 Bible Focus:
Make enough copies of the **"Comparing the Cults"** handouts (pp. 129-132) so every teenager gets one.

Investigating the Evidence

*   Gather materials for teenagers to create some sort of ad for the cults they're studying, like construction paper, pieces of poster board, scissors, markers, paper, pencils, and other art supplies.

Life Application:

*   Gather enough play money so that each teenager will get at least one bill. Make sure to bring some extra, just in case, and try to find bills that would be worth a lot if they were real. You'll be giving the play money to participants and won't get it back, so take your play money from an old board game that you have no intention of using anymore. Another place to check is a party superstore to see if they sell play money. If all else fails, create your own "funny money" on the computer and print it out—just be sure it's very obviously fake! If you can, find bills that have a really high denomination and would be very valuable if they were real.

- You'll also need to make copies of the **"Nicene Creed"** handout (p. 133), one per participant. If you'd prefer to use your own church's statement of faith instead, that's fine too—just be sure to make a copy for everyone. Also, make enough copies of the **"Confidence Builders"** handouts (pp. 134-135) so every participant gets one.

Leader Insight

Everyone these days seems to have some new take on Christianity. All teenagers have to do is turn on their TV or walk into a bookstore to hear someone explaining why their new interpretation of the gospel is so great. Turn on the news and you can hear about the Gospel of Judas and the Gospel of Thomas, or other gnostic scriptures that have been recently discovered and are giving us a whole new picture of Jesus. Dan Brown and his fictional *The Da Vinci Code* have convinced millions of people that even *Jesus himself* didn't believe he was God! Walk into Barnes & Noble and you'll notice that Deepak Chopra, the famous New Age guru, is writing book after book about his version of Jesus. Even Oprah is getting in on the game with her own church-free brand of vaguely Christian spirituality that she markets to millions of viewers every day.

The dangerous thing about all these fads is that it creates the impression that the truth of the gospel is just some big, fuzzy concept that there are a hundred different views about, and orthodox Christianity is just one more interpretation. Why should orthodox Christianity have a monopoly on the gospel? After all, it's just what a few people at a council sat down and said was right…right? Who's to say which version is correct? And every person or group claims to have some special interpretation that will show us the "real" Jesus.

In reality, these kinds of claims and attempts to subvert the gospel are nothing new. These movements have been popping up since the church was founded and we have a name for them: cults.

Some of your teenagers might have friends who are members of one of the cults that will be mentioned in this lesson. These friends may object to the word *cult* being used to describe their religion; they may claim to belong to just another Christian denomination—or are, in fact, the "true" Christianity. The important thing for your group, though, is to learn to recognize these false belief systems for what they really are and share the truth with their friends.

Any group whose core beliefs change or deny the fundamental teachings of orthodox Christianity and thus lie outside the realm of accepted Christian doctrine can be considered a cult, from Mormons to Jehovah's Witnesses to Postmodern Spiritualists to Christian Scientists and many other pseudo-Christian groups.

In the end, the only way teenagers will be able to pick out the imposters is to learn to recognize the real thing. Only by learning to know the real face of Jesus will they be able to guard themselves against the false ones.

tip   Interested in learning more about how cults compare to Christianity? Check out the Basic Beliefs Charts and the For Further Research suggestions on pages 136-145!

◊ Truth or Lies

As teenagers arrive, greet them warmly by name. Ask them to pair up with random partners while you distribute index cards and pencils, one per participant. Explain that partners are to quickly interview each other to discover unique facts about each other. But these are interviews with a twist—partners are really aiming to come up with two different kinds of information: truths and lies. Explain that they'll each need to write down two unique, true statements about their partner and also two totally made-up lies. The challenge is to make the two indistinguishable; they should try to make the true statements quite unbelievable and the lies very believable so that others will have a difficult time distinguishing between the two. And the real challenge here is for pairs to do this really quickly—in just five minutes.

> **tip** If teenagers need some help getting started, suggest that they talk about their families, pets, places they've lived, childhood experiences, and unusual hobbies. Also, if you have an uneven number of participants, either join the game yourself as someone's partner or allow one group to have three participants.

After five minutes, call time. Have pairs team up with other pairs to form groups of four. Within these groups, partners should "introduce" each other to the other pair by sharing the four statements they've written down about each other. The listening pair must try to determine which of the statements are lies. They won't have much time, though—allow just about one minute for each partner to be introduced and for the listening pairs to try to guess the lies.

Give everybody a chance to reveal the "answers" to their small group, then lead small groups in debriefing the game by asking them these questions:

- How did you try to figure out which statements were true and which weren't?

- How hard was it to guess which statements were true and which were lies?

- How do you think you would do playing this game with your best friend?

- What about with a total stranger? Why?

Have everyone gather back together as a large group and invite teenagers to share their reactions to the game. Ask volunteers to call out some of the outrageous truths or lies shared in their small groups.

THEN SAY:

You'd probably be able to spot lies easiest if you were playing with your best friend or a sibling, wouldn't you? Because the better you know a person, the easier it is to recognize the truth about that person and the easier it is to spot the lies. Let's find out how that applies to our study today on cults.

Back to Basics

To get an initial idea of your group's understanding of cults, ask:

- What are some cults that you've heard of?

- How would you define the term *cult* in your own words?

- What makes a religious group a cult?

SAY:

A cult is a religious group that claims to be Christian, but significantly changes or alters at least one of the basic beliefs that make up the core of Christianity: who God is, who Jesus is, the nature of the Bible, the nature of humanity, or the nature of sin. There are plenty of religions out there that don't claim or even pretend to be Christian—those are not cults. There are also a variety of Christian denominations and styles of worship, but as long as they agree on these basic points, they're not cults either.

Draw attention to the newsprint sheets you've hung on the wall.

SAY:

Let's figure out what the basic Christian beliefs about these things are. Help me get started.

Get suggestions from the group about what Christians agree on about these basic beliefs, and write their suggestions on the appropriate pieces of paper. Take just a minute or two per newsprint sheet—you'll add more to these lists later during the Life Application part of the study.

SAY:

Now let's see how these compare with what some of the cults teach.

 Bible Focus

Making the Cut

Explain that there are many different cults in the world and that there are too many to cover them all, so they'll just be looking at a few that are popular enough that lots of people know about them and consider them to be major "Christian" denominations. Remind them that a group is defined as a cult because it alters or denies some important aspect of basic Christian beliefs while still claiming to be Christian.

Distribute copies of the **"Comparing the Cults"** handouts (pp. 129-132), one per person, then have teenagers form small groups of three. Explain that it contains statements of belief from several cults that contradict the teaching of the Bible. Their mission will be to use the Scripture passages listed to find what the Bible really says.

Assign one cult to each small group to study and encourage them to have one person investigate each belief listed and then share their findings with the rest of their small group. (In addition to the Scriptures listed by specific false beliefs, draw teenagers' attention to the two Scripture passages listed at the start of the handout—John 1:1-18 and Philippians 2:5-11—making sure they read them too.) Give trios about 10 minutes to work, then call the groups back together for a review.

Ask the group:

- Were you surprised by any of the statements on your handout? Which ones?

- Have you ever heard any of these beliefs and ideas before? Where?

- What beliefs did you find that might be very attractive to people? What makes them attractive?

Investigating the Evidence

New and Improved!

SAY:

Now that you've seen a little bit of what some cults believe, let's look at what makes them attractive to people by making ads for them.

Make the project supplies available in a central location and explain that everybody should form new small groups of three or four; they should aim to be with different people than those who were in their trio for the "Making the Cut" activity.

> ### tip
> If you've got fewer than 16 participants, still have teenagers form teams of three or four, but just assign two or three of the cults. On the other hand, if you have a rather large group, create larger ad teams of five or six students each.

Explain that the new small groups will each be an "advertising team" for one of the cults on the handout. Assign a cult to each team, making sure that all four cults are covered. Then tell teams that their job will be to create some sort of an advertisement that promotes the key ideas of their cult in an appealing way—they could make a poster, a brochure, a mass mailing, a radio or TV commercial (or infomercial), a magazine or newspaper ad, and so on. Their ad can be serious, funny, or downright cheesy—whatever the team wants to create. Prompt teams to make sure they use their handouts to zero in on key ideas that might draw people to the cult. Challenge them to be certain that they include at least one of their assigned cult's beliefs that is a lie or a twist on biblical truth. When everyone's got the basic idea, have them get started. Warn them that they'll have to work fast—they only have about 10 minutes.

As teams work, wander around the room, encouraging teams and helping them get to work if they're stuck or need some help. When time is up, call everyone back together and ask each team to present their ad to the rest of the group.

After the presentations, applaud everyone for their efforts. Then ask the large group:

> **tip** If you have more than six or seven teams, you may want to consider having two or three ad teams group up to present their ads to each other rather than having every team present their ad to the large group.

- What are some of the attractions of each of these cults? (If needed, name each cult to guide the group's responses.)

- What lies can you identify in each of the ads?

- How do you know they're lies? Be specific.

SAY:

Sadly, if people believe the wrong things about God or that there is another way to him other than through Jesus, they will never know salvation.

Now that we've seen some pretty attractive reasons to believe those lies, let's imagine an advertisement that would attract people to follow the truth—one that would encourage people involved in cults to convert to true Christianity.

Invite suggestions from everyone on what they would put in such an ad.

Ask:

- In light of what we've been learning, what do you think is most attractive about Christianity?

- How would you try to encourage a cult follower to embrace the truth?

- How hard do you think it would be to convince a cult follower of the truth? Why?

Diving in Deeper

Pass out the play money, making sure everyone gets at least one bill.

As you do, **SAY:**
Here's your payment for the ads you just created.

Ask:

- What do you think of this money? How do you know it's fake?

- If you sincerely believed this money were real and you tried to spend it at a store, what would happen? Why?

Share that no matter how sincerely they might believe the money is real, their belief can't *make* it real. It is still fake money. Likewise, no matter how sincerely someone believes in the teachings of a cult, and no matter how attractive those teachings might seem, that doesn't make the teachings real. Explain that those beliefs are still worthless when it comes to a person's eternal salvation. Jesus doesn't give extra credit for sincerely believing in pretty lies.

SAY:

Bank tellers who have been trained in spotting counterfeit money can recognize it because they handle the real thing all the time. In reality, counterfeit money these days is a little more sophisticated than what I just gave you, but when you know the real thing so well, it's easy to spot a fake. The same thing is true about Christianity.

Ask:

- How can you tell if a religious group is a cult?

SAY:

If you have an intimate relationship with the "real thing"—Jesus—it will be much easier to spot the lies.

Give everyone copies of the **"Nicene Creed"** handout (p. 133) and tell them to glance through it. Explain that the Nicene Creed is a statement that early church fathers created as a way to help Christians understand the basic teachings of the Bible and identify false teachings. Or, if you'd prefer, pass out copies of your church's own doctrinal statement or some other simple summary of your church's basic beliefs.

Give teenagers a few minutes to read through the Nicene Creed or your church's statement of faith. Then draw everyone's attention back to the newsprint sheets on the wall that the group worked on during the Warm-Up part of the study.

Ask:

- How well did we do at listing the basic Christian beliefs?

- Is there anything we should change or add now that we've looked more closely at what the Bible says?

Take a few minutes to change or add to these beliefs based on the group's suggestions. Also, if there are important beliefs that you notice have been overlooked, add those to the lists as well. Be sure the group includes any essential biblical truths that distinguish orthodox Christianity from the teachings of cults.

Let's think about some ways that we can all get to know Jesus—the truth of Christianity—better.

Invite everyone to call out their ideas, and write them down on a dry-erase board. If nobody mentions spending time reading and studying the Bible, suggest it yourself.

SAY:

Jesus sent out his disciples in pairs to tell people about him. It's a good model. A partner can help us share the load, keep us accountable for our words and actions, and encourage and support us.

Explain that studying the Bible with a partner is a great way to discover the truth about what Christians believe. Encourage them to think about someone they would like to study the Bible with—a Bible buddy.

Also explain that another great way to grow in their faith as a confident Christian is to read a book that goes deeper in explaining and defending Christian beliefs. Give each student a copy of the **"Confidence Builders"** handouts (pp. 134-135) for suggestions on some great books and websites.

Have teenagers form Bible-buddy pairs and ask them to plan a time when they'll get together (or talk on the phone) to study the Bible. Encourage the pairs to pick a chapter or two of the Bible to study. If they aren't sure what to pick, suggest that the book of John is a great place to start. Or if they want to read a book, encourage them to read through the descriptions on the handout and to pick one they think looks interesting and make plans to read it and discuss what they've read each week.

If you think some of the teenagers in your group could benefit from a more mature Bible buddy or mentor, line up some adult partners or college students who would be willing to spend time studying the Bible with one or more of your young people.

After pairs have had a few minutes to make plans, call them back together. Tell them to keep their play money as a reminder of how they can spot counterfeits by getting to know the real thing. Suggest that they tape the play money to their mirror or in their locker, use a bill as a bookmark in their Bible, or put it someplace else where they will see it often.

Close the session in prayer. Pray that everyone in the group will follow through on their commitments to study the truth and that by doing so they will all get to know Jesus better and become more confident Christians. Pray also that teenagers would have the words of truth to share gently and lovingly with their friends who are trapped in false beliefs.

COMPARING THE CULTS

The following statements come directly from various cults, explaining what they believe. These are only some of the cults you might encounter, and only some of their beliefs. Many of these beliefs are common to other cults, though, and more and more of them are working their way into the minds of ordinary Christians who don't even realize that their faith is being compromised. So just because you hear one of these ideas coming from the mouth of someone who isn't a Jehovah's Witness or a Mormon doesn't mean it isn't a cult belief. For each statement you read, check out what the Bible says to find out the truth. Start by reading John 1:1-18 and Philippians 2:5-11. If you need more help, check out the other verses listed, too.

Jehovah's Witnesses say...	The Bible says...	Notes
"Jesus was a created spirit being, just as angels were spirit beings created by God. The fact is that Jesus is not God and never claimed to be." (www.watchtower.org)	John 10:30 Colossians 1:15-20	
"Michael the archangel is no other than the only-begotten Son of God, now Jesus Christ." (*New Heavens and a New Earth*, as summarized in *The Watchman Expositor*)	Romans 9:5 Hebrews 1:4-8, 13-14 Revelation 22:8-9	
"The Anointed (144,000) will be in heaven to reign with Jehovah God. The rest of the faithful Jehovah's Witnesses (not of the 144,000) will live forever on a paradise Earth." (*Let God Be True*, as summarized in *The Watchman Expositor*)	Isaiah 24:1-3; 51:6 Matthew 24:35 John 14:1-3	

Mormons say...	The Bible says...	Notes
"There is another Testament of Jesus Christ. The Book of Mormon, another Testament of Jesus Christ, is a companion volume of scripture to the Holy Bible and contains the account of the Savior's appearance in ancient America following his resurrection." (www.lds.org)	Proverbs 30:5-6 Revelation 22:18-19	
"It is the first principle of the Gospel to know for a certainty the character of God. ... He was once a man like us...God himself, the Father of us all, dwelt on an earth, the same as Jesus Christ himself did." (*Teachings of the Prophet Joseph Smith*, pp. 345-46)	Genesis 1:1 Isaiah 43:10 Hebrews 13:8 Revelation 1:8; 4:8	
"These are some of the blessings given to exalted people: They will become gods...They will have everything that our Heavenly Father and Jesus Christ have—all power, glory, dominion, and knowledge." (*Doctrines of Salvation*, 2:36)	Deuteronomy 6:4 Isaiah 43:10; 44:6; 45:5-6, 18, 22 1 Thessalonians 4:16-17	

Christian Science believers say…	The Bible says…	Notes
"If God, or good, is real, then evil, the unlikeness of God, is unreal." (Mary Baker Eddy, *Science and Health With Key to the Scriptures*)	Genesis 2:16-17; 3:4-5, 22 Ephesians 6:12 Hebrews 5:14	
"Man is incapable of sin, sickness, and death." (Mary Baker Eddy, *Science and Health With Key to the Scriptures*)	Romans 3:23; 5:12; 6:23	
"One sacrifice, however great, is insufficient to pay for the debt of sin. The atonement requires constant self-immolation on the sinner's part." (Mary Baker Eddy, *Science and Health With Key to the Scriptures*)	Romans 5:6-11; 6:5-10 Ephesians 2:8-9	
"God and man, Father and Son, are one in being." (Mary Baker Eddy, *Science and Health With Key to the Scriptures*)	Isaiah 43:10; 44:6; 45:5-6, 18, 22	

Unitarian Universalists say…	The Bible says…	Notes
"We believe that personal experience, conscience, and reason should be the final authorities in religion." (www.uua.org)	Acts 17:11 2 Timothy 3:14-15 1 John 4:1-3	
"Many of us honor Jesus, and many of us honor other master teachers of past or present generations, like Moses, or the Buddha." (www.uua.org)	John 14:6	
"Some Unitarian Universalists are nontheists and do not find language about God useful." (www.uua.org)	Genesis 1:1 Deuteronomy 6:4	
"Instead of salvation you will hear of our yearning for, and our experience of, personal growth, increased wisdom, strength of character, and gifts of insight, understanding, inner and outer peace, courage, patience, and compassion." (www.uua.org)	Romans 3:9, 23; 6:23 Ephesians 2:8-9	

THE NICENE CREED

The Nicene Creed is a statement of Christian faith that was first written out in 325 A.D. and is accepted by virtually every major denomination of Christianity (and not by the cults we've been studying). It lays out the core truths taught in the Bible and is fairly easy to memorize, even for people who can't read, so all Christians can have a handy reference for telling truth from heresy. It is not Scripture, but it is a handy reference.

We believe in one God, the Father, the Almighty, maker of heaven and earth, of all that is, seen and unseen.

We believe in one Lord, Jesus Christ, the only Son of God, eternally begotten of the Father, God from God, Light from Light, true God from true God, begotten, not made, of one Being with the Father.

Through him all things were made.

For us men and for our salvation he came down from heaven: by the power of the Holy Spirit he became incarnate from the Virgin Mary, and was made man.

For our sake he was crucified under Pontius Pilate; he suffered death and was buried.

On the third day he rose again in accordance with the Scriptures; he ascended into heaven and is seated at the right hand of the Father.

He will come again in glory to judge the living and the dead, and his kingdom will have no end.

We believe in the Holy Spirit, the Lord, the giver of Life, who proceeds from the Father and the Son.

With the Father and the Son he is worshipped and glorified.

He has spoken through the Prophets.

We believe in one holy catholic and apostolic Church.

We acknowledge one baptism for the forgiveness of sins.

We look for the resurrection of the dead, and the life of the world to come.

Amen.

CONFIDENCE BUILDERS

Books

- *The Apologetics Study Bible* (Holman Bible Publishers, 2007)—a great study Bible with excerpts written by dozens of the best Christian thinkers and apologists.

- *Jesus Among Other Gods* (Youth Edition) by Ravi Zacharias and Kevin Johnson (W Publishing, 2000)—a great comparison of Christianity with other major world religions, and why Jesus stands uniquely above them all.

- *The Case for Christ* (Youth Edition) by Lee Strobel and Jane Vogel (Zondervan, 2001)—an investigative reporter puts Christianity to the test.

- *The New Evidence That Demands a Verdict* by Josh McDowell (Thomas Nelson, 1999)—the classic apologetics resources, updated and revised for the 21st century.

- *Mere Christianity* by C.S. Lewis (Harper, 2001)—a fascinating and exciting defense of orthodox Christianity, "mere" Christianity.

- *Are All Religions One?* by Douglas Groothuis (InterVarsity Press, 1996)—exploring the question of whether all religions are the same at the core and whether Christianity really has the right to claim to truth.

- *The Kingdom of the Cults* by Walter Martin (Bethany House, 2003)—the ultimate resource on cults.

- *Fast Facts on False Teachings* by Ron Carlson and Ed Decker (Harvest House Publishers, 2003)—an easy-to-use resource for learning about false religions.

- *So What's the Difference?* by Fritz Ridenour (Regal Books, 2001)—how Christianity differs from 20 other major worldviews.

- *The Challenge of the Cults and New Religions* by Ron Rhodes (Zondervan, 2001)

CONFIDENCE BUILDERS...continued

Websites

- www.waltermartin.com (a resource on cults)

- www.josh.org (website of Josh McDowell Ministries)

- www.leestrobel.com (Lee Strobel's Investigating Faith website)

- rzim.org (website of Ravi Zacharias International Ministries)

BASIC BELIEFS CHART: Christianity

Use the following chart to compare the belief systems discussed in this book.

	God	Jesus	The World	Human Beings	Sin	The Afterlife	Religious Texts
CHRISTIANITY	God is the ruler of all and exists as one God in three persons: the Father, the Son, and the Holy Spirit. God is the eternal creator of the universe in which we live. God reveals himself to human beings through the Bible and through creation.	Jesus was 100 percent God and 100 percent man. He is God's Son and part of the Trinity. Jesus died on a cross and was resurrected for the forgiveness of sins.	The world was created by God.	Humans were created by God for relationship with him. Humans are separated from God by sin, but can find forgiveness through faith in Jesus.	All human beings are sinful and that sin separates them from God.	Human beings who have a faith relationship with Jesus will go to heaven when they die and spend eternity with God. Those who do not place their faith in Jesus will be separated from God in hell.	The Bible

BASIC BELIEFS CHART: Hinduism

Use the following chart to compare the belief systems discussed in this book.

	God	Jesus	The World	Human Beings	Sin	The Afterlife	Religious Texts
HINDUISM	God or "Brahman" is a universal spirit that has taken on many different forms. People are part of that spirit and the ultimate goal of Hindus is to be absorbed back into the spirit of Brahman.	Jesus was one of many of god's sons. He was a teacher or guru. He didn't rise from the dead.	The world was created by Brahman. Every living creature is believed to have a soul.	Humans came into existence through Brahman and are thought to be part of god like drops in the sea.	There really isn't such a thing as sin; however, a person's future depends entirely on his or her present behavior. Bad actions result in future suffering, experienced in the exact same measure (karma).	When a person dies, he or she returns to earth in the form of another living creature determined by karma. The only way to break this cycle of reincarnation is through philosophy or knowledge, works of religious observance, and devotion.	There are several religious texts in Hinduism. The Vedas (the oldest, written about 1000 B.C.) contain Hindu law, the Great Epics tell great stories, and the Puranas contain mythology from the medieval period.

Use the following chart to compare the belief systems discussed in this book.

	God	Jesus	The World	Human Beings	Sin	The Afterlife	Religious Texts
BUDDHISM	There is no god (or if there is, he is unknowable). However, there is a universal force that runs through all things.	Jesus was a man who had good teachings. He may have been an enlightened teacher. He was not God.	Zen Buddhists don't give an explanation for the world's existence. They believe people cannot definitively understand where the universe came from.	Individuality and desire are the source of suffering. By overcoming desire, humans can reach enlightenment.	There really is no such thing as sin. However, people can make themselves worse off and further from enlightenment through their thoughts and actions.	Nirvana (bliss) may be reached after complete enlightenment. Many Buddhists believe that one's consciousness will cease existing after death and the person becomes a part of the energy that makes up the universe.	The Tipitaka are the collected writings of Siddhartha Gautama (Buddha). Buddhists also refer to a variety of writings from enlightened teachers throughout the ages.

BASIC BELIEFS CHART: New Age Movement

Use the following chart to compare the belief systems discussed in this book.

	God	Jesus	The World	Human Beings	Sin	The Afterlife	Religious Texts
NEW AGE MOVEMENT	God is an impersonal force, sometimes called a consciousness or an energy. God is *all* and *all* is god. God is the life within all things.	Jesus was an enlightened teacher and is on the same level with other holy men such as Buddha (Buddhism) and Krishna (Hinduism). New Age adherents see Christ as a representative of the cosmic and divine.	The earth is a cosmic goddess, sometimes referred to as Mother Earth. Since all is one and god is all, the world and humankind are one and are both divine.	Humankind is god. Because humans are god, they have unlimited potential. Humans, as gods, can create their own realities.	Human beings do not have a sin problem; they have a problem of ignorance. Humans are ignorant or unaware of their divinity.	Through reincarnation, a person is eventually made perfect and ultimately reunited with the divine god-force. Dead people who are in a state of perfected enlightenment can be contacted via channeling for information and insight.	The New Age movement uses many different sources, such as the Bible and Levi Dowling's *The Aquarian Gospel of Jesus the Christ.* The New Age movement also adheres to new revelations from channeling.

Use the following chart to compare the belief systems discussed in this book.

	God	Jesus	The World	Human Beings	Sin	The Afterlife	Religious Texts
JUDAISM	God is one and is eternal. He cannot be divided into parts or beings in any way. God is the creator and has revealed himself and his will for us through the Law, the prophets, and the rabbis' teachings.	Jesus was a good teacher who taught things that were similar to the teachings of other rabbis of his day. He was not divine.	The world was created by God.	All human beings were created by God, but the Jews were chosen to be God's special people through whom he would bless the world.	People are not born sinful, but they do have the freedom to choose between right and wrong.	People who generally follow God's teachings and refrain from too much sinning have hope of the resurrection. Jewish teachings on the nature of the afterlife are diverse and somewhat vague.	The books of the Christian's Old Testament are considered God's Word. The teachings of the rabbis (the Talmud) hold a place of high importance as well.

Use the following chart to compare the belief systems discussed in this book.

	God	Jesus	The World	Human Beings	Sin	The Afterlife	Religious Texts
ISLAM	There is only one god, Allah, who has no equals. Nothing compares with Allah, as Muslims state in their cry, "Allah is greater."	Jesus was a very highly esteemed messenger of Allah. Jesus was one of the greatest prophets but was not God. Jesus did not die but "was made to appear so to them." Allah saved Jesus from the cross by raising him to himself before death.	The world was created by Allah in six days.	Humans were created by Allah to be basically good. They have a special responsibility to care for Allah's creation and are destined for heaven unless they disobey Allah.	Allah has given humans the choice to obey or disobey his laws. Disobedience is sin.	Muslims who perform all the essential obligations in worship with the proper attitude of total submission to Allah will go to paradise (heaven). All others go to hell, a place of everlasting torment.	The Koran is believed to be the final word of Allah given to humans. Muslims believe the angel Gabriel gave it directly to Muhammad and it alone is divinely inspired. The Hadith, collected sayings and acts of the prophet Muhammad, is an important text but is not considered divinely inspired.

BASIC BELIEFS CHART: Cults: Mormonism

Use the following chart to compare the belief systems discussed in this book.

	God	Jesus	The World	Human Beings	Sin	The Afterlife	Religious Texts
CULTS: MORMONISM	God was once a man and lived on "an earth." God is one of many gods.	Jesus lived as a sinless human to show people the way to earn their own exaltation.	The world was created by god so he could give his spirit children human life and the chance of eternal exaltation.	People are god's spirit children, placed on earth in human form to attain eternal exaltation.	Adam's sin actually fulfilled god's purpose of populating the earth. Humans must follow many laws to earn exaltation.	Faithful Mormon men will be exalted and become gods, ruling and populating their own earths. Women can be exalted only if sealed in marriage to a Mormon man.	The Bible, *Book of Mormon*, *Doctrine and Covenants*, *The Pearl of Great Price*

BASIC BELIEFS CHART: Cults: Jehovah's Witnesses

Use the following chart to compare the belief systems discussed in this book.

CULTS: JEHOVAH'S WITNESSES

God	Jesus	The World	Human Beings	Sin	The Afterlife	Religious Texts
God the Father is god alone. Jesus is god's first creation and is the same as Michael the archangel. The Holy Spirit is god's impersonal, active energy force.	Jesus is god's created son. Jesus was a perfect human being, but was not god. His death and resurrection earned humans the right to perfect life on earth.	The world was created by god as a paradise for perfect human existence.	Humans were created by god to live a perfect life on a paradise earth.	All human beings are sinful because of Adam's sin. Jesus' perfect human life and death gives humans the right to perfect life on a paradise earth, but people must earn that prize by living rightly.	Anointed people (144,000) will enjoy rebirth as god's spiritual children and rule with him in heaven. Other faithful Jehovah's Witnesses followers who obey all the laws have a chance to live forever on a paradise earth. All others are destroyed.	*The New World Translation of the Bible* and publications of the Watchtower Bible and Tract Society

For further research, check out the following resources.

Books

- *The Apologetics Study Bible* (Holman Bible Publishers, 2007)

- *Jesus Among Other Gods* (Youth Edition) by Ravi Zacharias and Kevin Johnson (W Publishing, 2000)

- *The Case for Christ* (Youth Edition) by Lee Strobel and Jane Vogel (Zondervan, 2001)

- *The New Evidence That Demands a Verdict* by Josh McDowell (Thomas Nelson, 1999)

- *Mere Christianity* by C.S. Lewis (Harper, 2001)

- *Are All Religions One?* by Douglas Groothuis (InterVarsity Press, 1996)

- *The Kingdom of the Cults* by Walter Martin (Bethany House, 2003)

- *Fast Facts on False Teachings* by Ron Carlson and Ed Decker (Harvest House Publishers, 2003)

- *So What's the Difference?* by Fritz Ridenour (Regal Books, 2001)

- *The Challenge of the Cults and New Religions* by Ron Rhodes (Zondervan Publishing House, 2001)

Christian Websites

- www.waltermartin.com (a resource on cults)

- www.josh.org (website of Josh McDowell Ministries)

- www.leestrobel.com (Lee Strobel's Investigating Faith website)

- rzim.org (website of Ravi Zacharias International Ministries)

- www.peterkreeft.com (a website with articles defending and explaining Christianity)

Books About Other World Religions

- *Am I a Hindu? The Hinduism Primer* by Ed Viswanathan (Halo Books, 1992)

- *Buddhism and Zen* by Nyogen Senzaki and Ruth Strout McCandless (North Point Press, 1987)

- *Being Jewish: The Spiritual and Cultural Practice of Judaism Today* by Ari L. Goldman (Simon & Schuster, 2000)

- *The House of Islam* (*Religious Life of Man*) by Kenneth Cragg and R. Marston Speight (Wadsworth Publishing Company, 1987)

Websites About Other World Religions

- www.hindunet.org (a Hinduism portal site)

- www.buddhanet.net (website of the Buddha Dharma Education Association)

- www.convert.org (official website of the Conversion to Judaism Resource Center)

- www.light-of-life.com (a comparison of Islam to Christianity from a Christian perspective)

- www.lds.org (official website of the Church of Jesus Christ of Latter-Day Saints)

- www.uua.org (official website of the Unitarian Universalist Association)